Homemade Dog Food Recipes

A practical, comprehensive, science-based guide to quick and easy healthy meals that won't break the budget, and supports your pet's well-being.

Jeanette Gower

Cover Photo by Shadows Farm Photography

Acknowledgements: Thanks to photographers Janice de Gennaro, Shadows Farm Photography, and Lesley Newcombe. Thanks also to 'editor in chief' Andy Ide. With special thanks to my sisters Frances and Anita, who have supported me so well in this journey.

PLATYPUS
PUBLISHING

Paperback: **978-1-968253-02-8**

Hardcover: **978-1-968253-16-5**

First edition published in Australia July 25.

Contents

Introduction

When I first brought home my retired greyhound, she was a gentle soul with a few quirks and some burgeoning health problems. Her racing days were behind her, but the wear and tear showed. Her coat was dull, her energy low, and she often dealt with digestive issues. She had been a nursing mom. It was clear she needed more than love; she needed a diet that could support her new, non-kennel lifestyle.

As someone who has owned and trained dogs in obedience since I was eight, who has bred champions, and worked on properties with working dogs, I thought I had a good handle on dog care. Yet, this greyhound taught me there was so much more to learn. After trying numerous commercial foods that promised the world but delivered little, I turned to homemade meals. The transformation was remarkable. Her coat grew shinier, her energy returned, and her digestive issues became a thing of the past. This was the moment I realized the power of homemade dog food.

This book is here to help you experience a similar transformation. Its purpose is simple: to guide you in preparing nutritious, affordable meals at home for your beloved dog. Whether you're new to dog ownership or not, this book aims to make meal preparation easy, even if you're not a natural in the kitchen. (That's certainly been me.)

I've lived with and trained dogs of all shapes and sizes. From Shetland Sheepdogs to Italian Greyhounds and Australian Cattle Dogs, each breed has taught me something new. My journey into homemade dog food began with that greyhound, but my experience spans decades.

As a breeder of Australian Stock Horses, I've also written extensively on equine care for horse magazines, and books on horse breeding which have been well-received. This rural background in animal care gives me a unique perspective, which bridges the gap between science and practical dog care.

Yes, until recently I had a full time job and I've raised a family. I understand your challenges. You're busy. You might have multiple dogs. You want the best for them, but budgets are tight and time is short. That's why this book focuses on practical, real-world solutions. Each recipe and tip fits into a busy lifestyle without breaking the bank.

What is special about this book is its focus on affordability and ease. There's no need for exotic ingredients or complicated techniques. Instead, you'll find scientifically backed advice tailored for your lifestyle. Each chapter is designed for confidence in the kitchen, even if you're starting from scratch.

The book is structured to guide you through every step. Nutrition can be confusing with so much conflicting information. We'll start with the basics, helping you understand what your dog truly needs. From there, we'll dive into diets tailored for different life stages and health concerns. You'll learn how to select budget-friendly ingredients that don't skimp on quality.

I encourage you to engage with the content. Try the recipes and see what works best for your dog. Keep a journal of your dog's journey to track improvements in health and happiness. Bookmark pages to come back to.

By applying the guidance in this book, you can expect noticeable improvements. Your dog will likely have a shinier coat, better digestion, and more energy. You'll find yourself less stressed at meal times, knowing exactly what's going into your dog's bowl. Most importantly, you'll gain confidence in your ability to provide for your dog's nutritional needs.

To wrap up, let me leave you with this: the journey to better health for your dog through homemade meals is incredibly rewarding. It's a chance to bond, to learn, and to make a real difference in your dog's life. I've seen it with my original greyhound, and more recently with my very picky dachshund who graces these pages! I know you can achieve the same. Together, let's make meal times a source of joy and health.

Welcome to the rewarding path of homemade dog food.

Holly my retired greyhound, in the peak of health,
doing zoomies around the backyard.

The Author with adopted greyhound, Holly

Chapter 1

Why homemade?

Feeding your dog shouldn't feel like guesswork.

T here's a reason you're holding this book.

Maybe you've watched your dog scratch endlessly at ears that never quite settle. Maybe their energy's dipped. Maybe their coat has lost its shine.

Or maybe, just maybe, you took one look at the back of a kibble packet and realized you didn't understand half of what was in it.

And that was your turning point.

Feeding them shouldn't feel like hoping for the best.

It should feel like what it is, an act of care.

And in many households now, that means *bringing the bowl back to homemade*. Preparing food with ingredients you can pronounce. Using what you already have in your fridge and pantry. Knowing what's going in, and why.

This book isn't about guilt. It's not here to say, "You've been doing it wrong."

It's here to say: *You have options*. And they're good ones.

The case for homemade

Commercial dog food has its place. It's convenient, shelf-stable, and engineered to meet minimum nutritional standards. But minimum doesn't mean optimal. And over time, for many dogs, that gap becomes obvious.

Some begin to develop chronic issues; itchy skin, digestive upset, anxiety, joint problems. For others, it's more subtle: weight creeping on, dull coat, a sluggishness that doesn't match their years.

And then there's trust. With pet food recalls becoming alarmingly common, and labels that use vague terms like "meat by-product," owners are increasingly asking: *What am I really feeding?*

Homemade food puts the answers back in your hands.

Budget: The quiet win

The idea that homemade feeding is "expensive" is one of the most persistent myths in the dog world.

Yes, it can be, if you're making grass-fed bison tartare with organic blueberries two times a week. But practical homemade feeding, the kind this book supports, uses:

- Inexpensive cuts of meat (chicken necks, lamb hearts, tinned sardines)
- Affordable fillers like oats, pumpkin, rice, and lentils
- Leftovers repurposed wisely
- Smart batching, freezing, and storage to reduce waste

Over time, many owners find that making food at home either matches or undercuts the cost of premium kibble or wet food in a can, and drastically reduces vet visits tied to diet-related issues.

Responsibility and rhythm

Feeding your dog at home takes a little time to begin with. It takes thought. But it also builds something you won't get from scooping dry pellets into a bowl. It builds rhythm.

Dogs *know* when you're cooking for them. They watch. They sniff. They sit by the bench like tiny supervisors. And when that food goes down, there's a kind of quiet satisfaction on both sides. You made it. They trust it.

That rhythm? That's a form of care. Just like brushing them. Just like walking them.

And here's the thing: feeding this way doesn't have to be perfect. It doesn't have to be fancy. It just has to be considered.

Intentional.

That's what this book helps you do.

Not just for the "foodie dog mum"

There's a misconception that only people with a lot of time, money, or Pinterest boards feed homemade.

That's not who this book is for.

This book is for the *busy parent* whose dog is their child's best mate. The *working tradie* who wants to do right by their kelpie. The *retired couple* living on a budget who want to support their senior dog's joints without another $120 bag of prescription food, or the rural farmer with multiple working dogs.

It's also for the beginner who doesn't yet know what a "complete and balanced" dog diet is, and isn't ashamed to admit it.

Wherever you're starting from, you're welcome here.

What this book isn't

Let's get this clear upfront:

- This book isn't a raw-feeding manifesto.

- It's not anti-vet.

- And it's not pushing extreme dietary philosophies.

Instead, it's about giving you a range of practical, evidence-aligned options, so you can make thoughtful decisions that suit *your* dog, *your* lifestyle, and *your* budget.

Whether you want to go fully homemade, mix-feed, or just learn to read a pet food label with a sharper eye, this book will walk you through it, without judgement.

Where we're going

In the chapters ahead, you'll find:

- Simple explanations of canine nutrition (without the jargon)

- A range of feeding styles, from slow-cooked to raw and everything in between

- Life-stage diets tailored for puppies, adults, seniors, and working dogs

- Special recipes for dogs with sensitive guts, dental needs, or anxiety

- Natural boosters and minor remedies, so food becomes your first line of support

- Realistic, flexible meal plans, even when life gets chaotic

And most importantly, you'll get confidence. Confidence to feed well, spend wisely, and care deeply.

Action Step:

Have a quick look in your pantry and fridge. What do you already have that's dog-safe? (Think: plain rice, frozen veggies, eggs, tinned sardines.) You might be closer to a homemade meal than you realise.

Energetic, happy dogs - Indi the Whippet and Evie the Dachshund.

Chapter 2

Real food, real dogs

W e don't eat the same thing every day, from a bag, stored in a plastic tub in the laundry.

We don't live well on ultra-processed pellets packed with mystery proteins and artificial vitamins.

And neither do dogs.

Real food with actual ingredients, fresh and identifiable, is as essential for dogs as it is for us. It's not a luxury. It's not a fad. It's a return to something we once knew instinctively: animals thrive on food that makes sense to their bodies.

And deep down, most owners know this. They just haven't been shown how simple it can be.

What do we mean by "real food"?

Let's keep it plain. Real food is food that still looks like food. It's meat, vegetables, whole grains, and oils. It's food you could eat yourself if you had to, though you'd probably want to season it first.

It's also:

- Recognisable: Chicken thigh, not "meat by-product."

- Ingredients you know are not contaminated by chemicals or hormones: Did you know that horses which are slaughtered for tinned pet food do not have the same regulatory requirements as horse meat for human consumption? "Dogger" horses may have had anti-parasitic drugs, soundness medications, sedation or regulatory hormones administered, prior to ending up in the auction yard.

- Minimal: No synthetic preservatives, colourings, or lab-formulated binding agents.

- Digestible: Gently cooked or raw, not blasted under high heat into brown pebbles.

- Purposeful: Each ingredient does something, protein to build muscle, fats for skin and energy, fibre to support digestion.

Real food doesn't need to be exotic or expensive. It just needs to be *intentional*.

Dogs were made for it

Dogs, like us, are adaptive omnivores. Their ancestors didn't chase down wheat fields or dine exclusively on meat. They ate all parts of their catch. They scavenged, they foraged, and they ate scraps from human settlements. And they didn't necessarily eat every day!

Their stomachs are robust, but not immune to poor feeding. Dogs can handle variety. They benefit from it. Their bodies know what to do with lightly cooked meat, eggs, rice, pumpkin, oily fish. These aren't strange foods to them, they're foundational.

What trips dogs up is excess and imbalance. Too many fillers. Too many additives. Too little real nutrition.

Homemade meals give you back the steering wheel.

How real food shows its impact

When dogs shift to real food, owners often report the same three things:

- Energy stabilises. No more wild sugar spikes from high-carb kibble.

- Skin clears. Fewer ear infections, hotspots, itching, or smelly coats.

- Digestion improves. Smaller, firmer stools. Less gas. Fewer upset tummies.

Over time, you also tend to see:

- Healthier weight

- Bright eyes

- Softer coats

- Fewer vet visits for chronic, low-level issues

That's not wishful thinking. That's what happens when a body gets what it needs.

But what about balance?

This is where many owners get nervous. They worry they'll "mess it up" or that a vet will scold them for not feeding an ""Approved-labelled kibble. The fear of doing it wrong holds a lot of people back from doing it better.

Here's the truth: yes, nutritional balance matters. But it's not fragile. You don't have to hit 100% every day, just like you don't panic if your child eats plain toast for dinner now and then.

Dogs benefit from nutritional variety over time, not perfection at every meal. This book will show you how to get that variety, across ingredients, prep styles, and life stages, without needing charts or spreadsheets.

The aim is not to replace science with guesswork. It's to *apply* science using ingredients you recognise and routines that fit into real life.

Why real doesn't mean complicated

Somewhere along the way, "natural" and "homemade" started sounding like code for high-maintenance. As if real feeding was only for people with a chef's hat and a free afternoon.

But here's the reality: feeding your dog real food can be as simple as this: Boil rice + add tinned sardines + stir in frozen spinach + crack an egg.

Done.

Batch cook on a Sunday and portion it out. Or mix and match based on what's in your fridge. You don't need a formula memorised. You need a handful of go-to options and a bit of guidance. That's what this book will offer. And after working through this book, you should have a comprehensive understanding which will enable you to mix, match and substitute to you and your dog's liking.

Kibble isn't the villain, but it's not the hero either

Kibble is a commercial convenience. It exists because it's cheap to make, easy to store, and shelf-stable for years. That doesn't make it evil, but it doesn't make it ideal, either.

The goal isn't to create anxiety every time you open a kibble bag.

The goal is to help you understand the limits of what processed food can do, and to fill those gaps with better choices.

For some, that'll mean transitioning to 100% homemade. For others, it may be mix-feeding, kibble in the morning, and homemade at night. Either way, you're lifting the quality of what goes into your dog's body.

Even one homemade meal a day can make a difference.
Example:

- Brown rice

- Frozen peas

- Tinned tuna (in spring water)

- Eggs

- Plain Greek yoghurt

We'll build from there in the chapters ahead.

Action Step:

Make a short list of 5 foods in your pantry or freezer that are safe for your dog. You're likely halfway to a homemade meal already.

Senior lookalikes, Holly and Jasper (R)

Chapter 3

Meet your dog's nutritional needs

What dogs need to thrive

F eeding well starts with understanding *what* your dog actually needs to thrive, not just survive. And here's the first truth: dogs don't need trends, gimmicks, or grain-free marketing spin.

They need nutrients. Real, balanced, digestible nutrients. Delivered in a way their body can use.

This chapter will break it down for you.

The five pillars of canine nutrition

Dogs require the same foundational elements we do. The difference is in the ratios, not the ingredients.

1. Protein: The builder

Essential for muscle maintenance, immune function, and cellular repair.

- Sources: Chicken, turkey, beef, lamb, (and other meats) sardines (and other fish), eggs

- Need-to-know: Animal protein is the gold standard. It contains all essential amino acids dogs require.

- Budget tip: Use cheaper cuts, offal, and tinned fish in rotation.

2. Fat: The fuel

Primary energy source for dogs. Also supports hormone health and skin condition.

- Sources: Chicken skin, fish oil, egg yolks, beef fat, flaxseed (linseed) oil

- Need-to-know: Dogs don't get heart disease from fat the way humans do. Fat is crucial.

- Watch for: Too much fat too fast can upset sensitive tummies. Introduce gradually.

3. Carbohydrates: The filler (fibre source)

Not essential, but incredibly useful. Dogs don't actually *require* carbs. Carbs can bulk meals, provide fibre, and support gut bacteria.

- Sources: Brown rice, oats, pearl barley, sweet potatoes, pumpkin, lentils and pulses (peas, chickpeas, beans)

- Need-to-know: Choose slow-release carbs over refined grains. Dogs digest them well when cooked.

- Budget tip: Rice is a great base: cheap, easy to prepare, and gut-soothing.

4. Vitamins and minerals: The fine tuners

These regulate everything from bone growth to nerve function. Most come from variety, not pills.

- Sources: Liver (vitamin A, iron), sardines (vitamin D, calcium), leafy greens (spinach, broccoli, green beans), eggshell powder

- Need-to-know: Balance happens over time, not every meal. Rotate for variety and balance.

- Avoid: Overdoing supplements. More isn't better.

5. Water: The Forgotten Essential

Dogs can go longer without food than without water.

- Need-to-know: Real food is naturally hydrating. Kibble (and to a lesser extent canned food) is dry, so dogs on commercial diets often drink more, but absorb less.

Tip: Bone broth is a great hydration booster for fussy drinkers. Save your cooking liquids.

Let me tell you a short story of my New Zealand friend's experience. He had a wonderful corgi, Bronie, who used to play in the river alongside their house, and drink from it regularly. Over time she stopped doing this, and would only drink from their tap. He thought it was due to her ageing.

But one day a letter arrived, stating that the river water was polluted and unsuitable for domestic or agricultural use. His dog knew!

Life stage nutrition: What changes?

While the basics stay the same, *how much* and *what ratio* of nutrients your dog needs will shift with age, activity, and condition.

- Puppies: Need more protein and fat for growth. Frequent meals. Calcium monitored carefully.

- Adults: Focus on maintenance. Balance energy needs with exercise levels.

- Seniors: Prioritise digestibility. Boost joint-supporting nutrients (e.g. omega-3s, glucosamine-rich bone broth).

- Pregnant/Nursing Dogs: Higher calories, high-quality fats, steady calcium.

- Working Dogs: More fat and calories to meet demand. Electrolyte support helps too.

We'll walk through each of these in dedicated chapters later.

What about "complete and balanced"?

You'll see this phrase everywhere, especially on pet food packaging. But here's the thing:

"Complete and balanced" means that food meets *minimum nutritional requirements* set by the national standards body in your country. (The AAFCO (Association of American Feed Control Officials), PFIA (Pet Food Industry, Australia) and is highly regulated in the UK by FSA (Food Standards Agency).

While many dogs thrive on kibble and / or canned pet food only, it doesn't mean it's the *best* your dog can get.

Standards are often based on synthetic additives designed to compensate for what's lost in processing. Many are not bio-available.(does not have an active effect in the body.) That's not a problem in homemade food made from fresh, diverse ingredients.

What matters more is:

- Ingredient quality

- Digestibility

- Variety over time

If you feed with intention, use whole foods, and rotate your ingredients. You'll meet your dog's needs without chasing your tail.

Note: Conflicts of interest can occur from vets who promote certain packaged dog food because selling them increases their profits. Commercial dog food manufacturers compete aggressively to win over sales through vets and pet store owners.

It is thought that vets make at least 15% of their revenue from packaged dog food or prescription dog food. Corporate takeovers are climbing, especially of pet food and veterinary chains, leading to intense lobbying for your dollar through advocating, marketing and advertising.

Vets and pet store chains then recommend certain products, even though they have had very little nutritional training!

For more information on what is actually in commercial dog foods, labelling, and common myths about packaged foods, go to https://www.healthydogtreats.com.au/commercial-dogtreats-truth/

The confidence to feed

You don't need to become a pet nutritionist. You just need to understand the basics, stay thoughtful, and feed like you care, which, clearly, you do.

This book won't drown you in figures. Instead, it will give you:

- Real-world recipes and ratios

- Ingredient substitutions based on budget and availability

- Checklists and sample plans to keep meals on track

Action Step:

Write down three protein sources and three carb sources your dog has eaten in the past week. Is there variety? If not, no panic. We'll build it in slowly over the coming chapters.

Chapter 4

How to use this book

T his book isn't a program. It's not a diet plan. It's a guide, with flexibility to start you off, or give you confidence in the kitchen.

You might be:

- Switching off kibble completely

- Mixing homemade meals with store-bought options

- Trying to cook one fresh meal a day to ease your dog's skin, gut, or weight issues

- Or simply learning what's actually in pet food and wondering if there's a better way

Wherever you are, this book is written to support you *without judgement, overwhelm, or pressure*. It's not all-or-nothing. It's real-world.

Follow it front to back, or jump around.

Each section is designed to stand alone but build logically.

- **Part 1: Getting Started**
  If you're new to homemade feeding, this is your base camp. It'll show you what to feed, how to transition, and how to set up your kitchen without spending a fortune.

- **Part 2: Feeding Styles**
  Whether you prefer cooking, mixing, or going raw, this section breaks down the pros and cons so you can find what suits your household.

- **Part 3: Special Diets and Life Stages**
  Because a six-month-old working dog doesn't need the same food as a 13-year-old chihuahua. This section will help you fine-tune for life stage, lifestyle, and medical needs.

- **Part 4: Practical Feeding and Storage**
  Batch-prepping, freezing, portioning, travel. This is the nuts-and-bolts of keeping it all manageable.

- **Part 5: Natural Remedies and Boosters**
  Everyday kitchen remedies, bone broths, and homemade additions to gently support common health issues.

- **Part 6: Recipes**
  Clear, flexible recipes broken into meals and treats. Each one includes prep method, life-stage suitability, portion suggestions, and freezer tips.

- **Appendices**
  Quick-reference charts, conversions, glossary of ingredients, and commonly asked questions.

Who this book is for

This is for dog owners who want better food on a budget. Not dog chefs. Not influencers. Not nutritionists in disguise.

This is for:

- Families juggling school drop-offs and budget shopping

- Retirees watching their dog's health and budget

- First-time owners who want to do it right

- Seasoned dog people who are tired of spending hundreds on vet-approved brands their dog won't touch

You won't need fancy appliances. You won't need perfect ratios every day. You'll just need a little time, a handful of ingredients, and a willingness to try.

Don't worry about getting it perfect

If you're the type who worries you'll mess it up, breathe. Dogs are adaptable, forgiving creatures. Homemade feeding doesn't have to be precise to be powerful.

This book is structured so you can:

- Try one new idea at a time

- Mix and match ingredients based on what's on sale

- Choose a feeding style that fits your lifestyle

- Learn to recognise when your dog is thriving or when something needs tweaking

And if you ever need to shift back to store-bought temporarily? That's fine. This isn't a purity test. It's a toolkit.

Friendly tip for readers:

When in doubt, choose the simpler ingredient list. If you can't pronounce half of it, your dog probably doesn't need it either!

Building your own plan

By the time you finish this book, you'll have everything you need to:

- Understand your dog's nutritional needs

- Choose your feeding style

- Shop with a list

- Prep meals for a day, a week, or a month

- Adjust recipes for different ages and health needs

- Supplement naturally, when needed

- Feel confident you're doing right by your dog

You can follow the full meal plans at the back, or just take one idea and run with it.

Action Step:

Take a moment to jot down your goal. Not "perfect dog food." Something simpler. Maybe it's "less itching," "more energy," or "more control over what goes in the bowl." That's your north star. Let's build toward it, one meal at a time.

Holly, a gentle soul, at the opening of our local dog park.

Part I

Getting Started

Pearl, the farm whippet.

Chapter 5

Transitioning from kibble and commercial dog foods

A step-by-step guide

W hether you're feeding dry pellets from a bulk bag or spooning out a can of lamb and "gravy," moving to homemade takes a little planning. Not because dogs resist real food. They don't. It's because their bodies, like ours, need time to adapt.

A fast switch from processed food to fresh can upset their digestion, not because fresh food is a problem, but because the gut needs time to adjust its enzymes and bacteria. It's like taking a break from sugar and coffee. You'll feel better, but maybe not on day one.

How to make that shift without the stress

Start with the 'why'

Dogs fed commercial food, especially kibble, are used to ultra-processed meals. The formulas are dense, dehydrated, and full of binding agents that your dog's digestive system has adapted to over time. Homemade meals are different:

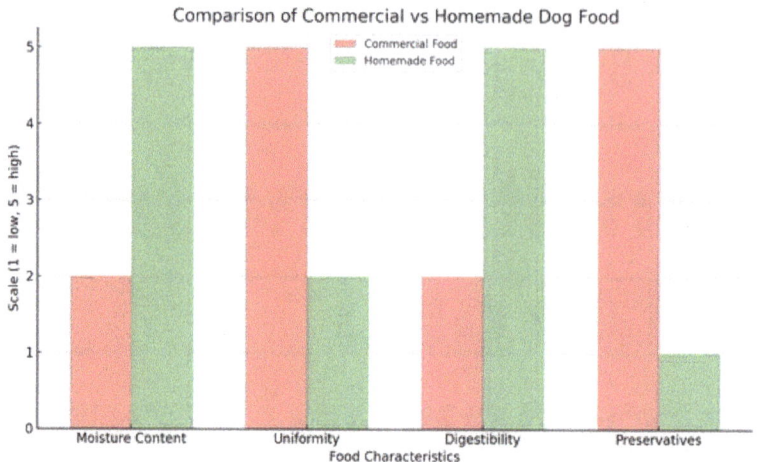

Comparison of Commercial vs Homemade Dog Food

Your dog's body needs to "relearn" how to break down real food efficiently. Going too fast can lead to runny stools, gurgly tummies, or a few days of confusion. Slow and steady always wins here.

Canned food vs. kibble. Does the transition change?

A little, yes. Kibble-fed dogs tend to need a gentler pace. Their guts are used to dry, concentrated food. Their water intake, chewing habits, and stool volume may all shift dramatically with real food.

Canned-fed dogs are often halfway there already. Canned food has higher moisture and softer textures, so the leap to homemade may be quicker. That said, it's still processed, so ingredient variety and balance are often lacking. Either way, this guide works.

The 7-Day transition framework

Here's a sensible default for most adult dogs. (Puppies and seniors may need a slightly slower pace.)

Day 1–2:
Feed 75% commercial food + 25% homemade.
Start with something mild: boiled chicken, rice, a spoonful of pumpkin.

Day 3–4:
50% commercial food + 50% homemade.
Include a second protein source (e.g. sardines, eggs) and a vegetable like zucchini or green beans.

Day 5–6:
25% commercial food + 75% homemade.

Start introducing oils (olive or fish), bone broth, or a small spoon of plain yoghurt.

Day 7:
100% homemade, provided digestion has stayed stable.

Gentle foods for first meals

Think: soft, digestible, and low-risk.

Good options:

- Boiled chicken or turkey

- Steamed carrots or pumpkin

- Tinned sardines in spring water

- Scrambled eggs (plain)

- Bone broth (no onion, no salt)

- White rice or oats

Avoid rich ingredients like liver or fatty meats until digestion has settled.

Monitor the transition

You're watching for:

- Stool consistency (soft is okay; watery or mucousy isn't)

- Gas or bloating

- Appetite or behaviour changes

If your dog is well but has loose stools, pause and hold the mix at the current ratio for a couple of days. There's no rush.

For sensitive or older dogs

Go slower. Even 10% per week if needed.

Older dogs or those with digestive issues benefit from:

- Blended meals (easy on the gut)

- Added probiotics (plain yoghurt or vet-recommended powders)

- Bone broth to soothe the stomach and encourage hydration

Always transition on a calm week, not when you're moving house, going on holidays, or just wormed them.

Can you go back if it doesn't work? Absolutely. You can pause. You can mix-feed. You can try again later.

There's no medal for fastest transition. The goal is a long-term shift that feels sustainable, not a crash course or a sudden change.

Action Step:

Pick your first transition day. Circle it on your calendar. Check what you already have in the fridge or freezer. Then write down your plan for Days 1–3. A little structure goes a long way.

Evie the dachshund. She is always busy.

Chapter 6

Understanding your dog's nutritional needs

Key signs

Y ou don't have to be a vet to know when something's off. You don't need a spreadsheet to feed your dog well, either.

But you do need to understand a few key signs, a few basic principles, and how to adjust when things shift.

Feeding isn't just about recipes. It's about watching. Noticing. Tweaking. And this chapter is here to help you read your dog like a good stockman reads a paddock, calmly, clearly, and with quiet confidence.

Signs your dog is thriving

No guessing needed. When food is working, your dog will show it.

Look for:

- Bright eyes

- Soft, shiny coat (not greasy, not dry)

- Firm, consistent stools

- Steady energy. Calm when resting, keen when active

- Good appetite (but not obsessive begging)

- Clean ears and minimal itching

- Fresh breath and white teeth

That's a balanced dog.

When something's off

If your dog is experiencing any of these, something may be lacking, or in excess:

- Runny or inconsistent stools

- Dry, flaky skin or a dull coat

- Persistent gas or bloating

- Weight gain or loss without explanation

- Low energy or sudden hyperactivity

- Ear infections, hot spots, or paw licking

These signs can point to imbalances in protein, fat, fibre, or even trace minerals. They can also be allergy-related.

That doesn't mean your whole feeding plan is wrong. It just means you need to adjust, one thing at a time.

Common imbalances (and simple fixes)

- Too much protein: Strong-smelling stools, possible hyperactivity
  Try blending in more complex carbs (oats, sweet potato)

- Too little fat: Dull coat, flaky skin, low energy
  Add sardine oil, flaxseed oil, or small amounts of cooked fat

- Too many carbs: Weight gain, sluggishness, large stools
  Reduce rice/potato and boost lean protein. Dogs don't actually *require* carbs.

- Lack of fibre: Soft or inconsistent stools
  Add pumpkin, green beans, or psyllium husk in small doses

- Calcium Imbalance: Soft stools, joint stiffness in puppies
  Add crushed eggshell (dried and ground) or rotate in sardines with bones

How often should you change the menu?

Dogs thrive on routine, but not monotony. Too much of one protein, for example, can cause intolerances over time.

A good rhythm looks like:

- Switching main proteins every 2–3 weeks

- Rotating veggies and carb sources weekly

- Using organ meats 1–2 times per week (not daily)

- Adding bone broth or fresh boosters a few times a week

Think of it as a roster, not a recipe. Feed variety *over time*, not necessarily at every meal.

How much to feed?

This varies. But here's a simple formula to start with:

- 2–3% of your dog's body weight per day (split across 1–2 meals)

  - Smaller dogs tend to need closer to 3%

  - Larger or less active dogs closer to 2%

  - Puppies and working dogs may need more (4–6%)

For a 20kg (44lb) adult dog:

- 2.5% = 500g (1lb2oz)of food per day

- Made up of approx. 70% protein/fat, 20% carbs, 10% veggies

You'll get a full feeding calculator in the appendices.

Watch the dog, not the bowl

Every dog is different. Some will thrive on rice. Others need oats. Some love sardines; others turn their nose up. That's normal.

Feeding well isn't about being rigid. It's about watching your dog:

- Are they licking their paws more?

- Gaining weight slowly?

- Throwing up bile first thing in the morning?

These are all clues. Your dog's body is speaking. This book will help you learn its language.

Action Step:

Spend three days noting your dog's energy, stool consistency, coat condition, and appetite. These are your "baseline" signs. You'll refer back to them each time you change or adjust a meal plan.

Screwtop containers can be ideal for small meals.

Chapter 7

Pantry staples and kitchen tools

What to keep on hand

Homemade feeding doesn't need a fancy kitchen or gourmet gadgets. What it does need is *preparation*. That means a pantry with the right staples, and a few basic tools that help you cook, portion, and store meals without fuss.

This chapter is your no-nonsense setup guide: what to keep on hand, what's worth buying, and what you can skip entirely.

Start with what you've got

Before you buy anything, check your own pantry. Chances are, you already have several dog-safe staples ready to go.

Here are a few examples:

- Grains: Brown rice, oats, barley, couscous

- Proteins: Tinned tuna or sardines (in spring water), eggs, leftover cooked meats

- Veggies: Frozen peas, pumpkin, sweet potato, carrots, green beans. Frozen vegs are actually really good as they are often picked at a prime time so still have all the nutrients

- Fats and Oils: Olive oil, flaxseed oil, coconut oil

- Boosters: Apple cider vinegar, turmeric, natural yoghurt

The key is to make the best of what's already in your kitchen. Don't rush out to stock specialty items unless you *know* you'll use them.

The budget-friendly pantry list

Here's a practical starter list you can build from. (Fresh, pre-cooked or frozen.) If possible buy when on special, or in bulk to save on costs. Farmers markets and fish markets, often provide bulk buying benefits. Divide up into usable sizes before freezing.

Pantry staples

Proteins:	Vegetables:
Chicken thighs or necks	Pumpkin (tinned or fresh)
Beef mince or stew cuts	Carrots
Lamb hearts or liver (once a week)	Broccoli
Sardines or mackerel in water	Spinach (chopped, frozen is fine)
Eggs	Zucchini
	A variety of frozen chopped veggies
Carbs:	**Boosters:**
Brown rice	Natural yoghurt (no sugar or xylitol)
Rolled oats	Turmeric
Sweet potato	Bone broth (homemade or clean store-
Pasta (plain, unsalted)	bought. No onion or garlic)
Pearl barley	Crushed eggshell (for calcium)
	Apple cider vinegar
Healthy Fats:	
Tinned fish	
Olive oil	
Coconut oil	
Flaxseed (linseed) ground	

In some cases, buying carefully-chosen ready-made products is smarter, safer, and time-saving.

Bone broth

Can be made or bought. Homemade bone broth is wonderful if you have time (plus cheap). However, unsalted, vet-approved, dog-specific bone broths are fine to buy for convenience.

Warning: Always read the label. No onions, garlic, excess salt, or seasoning!

Purees (pumpkin, sweet potato, etc.)

Canned 100% pure pumpkin or sweet potato purée (with no additives) is completely fine to buy rather than make fresh every time. It's stable, easy to store, and very consistent in texture.

Tip: Double-check it's "pure pumpkin" not "pumpkin pie filling" (which often contains sugar and nutmeg, which are unsafe.

Collagen, probiotics, supplements

Generally easier to buy. Supplements like collagen powders, fish oil capsules, and probiotic chews are hard to replicate safely at home. Always pick dog-specific brands or check with a holistic vet.

Smart rule: If you can make it fresh, easily and safely, homemade is beautiful. If precision matters (milk, minerals, supplements), or if time is tight, buy trusted ready-made versions and focus your energy where it counts most (meal prepping, training, bonding!).

Stock what you'll use. Keep it simple, especially at the start.

What about supplements?

In most cases, a varied, real-food diet doesn't require a lot of extras. But here are a few that may be worth considering, especially for seniors or sensitive dogs:

- Probiotics: plain yoghurt or vet-approved powders

- Fish oil: for skin, coat, joints

- Kelp powder: trace minerals and iodine

- Eggshell calcium: if feeding boneless meals long-term

You'll learn when (and if) to add these later in the book.

Tools you'll actually use

Skip the gadgets. Focus on the basics.

- Large saucepan or slow-cooker

- Sharp knife, + cutting board

- Measuring cup or digital scale

- Glass containers or BPA-free tubs

- Freezer bags (for bulk storage)

- Blender or stick mixer (optional, for soft meals or purees)

- Large measuring jug

- Wooden stirrer, ladle, large spoons, potato masher

- Ice cube trays, muffin trays (for freezing broth, pre-portioned boosters)

- Use a kitchen scale for accuracy, at least when starting out. You'll quickly get the feel.

You don't need to spend hundreds setting up. In fact, most owners do just fine with what they've already got.

How to store ingredients

Fresh food needs a little more planning, but it also teaches rhythm. Before long you will have created a meaningful habit.

- Dry storage: Keep grains, tinned goods, and oils in a cool place

- Glass jars: Great for storing ground eggshells, flax, or dehydrated treats

Fridge storage:

- Store up to 3 days of food in airtight containers

- Use glass jars or BPA-free tubs for freshness. If it doesn't have a lid, wrap in aluminium foil.

- Keep meal portions separate for easy grab-and-go

Freezer storage:

- Freeze individual meals or bulk portions for 2–3 weeks (or up to 2 months in airtight packaging)

- Muffin trays for single-dog servings

- Ziplock bags: flattened for fast thawing. Lie side by side, like books.

- Silicone ice cube trays for small dogs or toppers

- Glass containers for long-term, and organised

More on containers:

Plastic containers might seem convenient, but they can come with hidden downsides. Many plastics contain BPA or phthalates, which can leach into food over time, especially when heated, frozen, or reused often. Even BPA-free plastics can break down or retain odours and fats from oily foods like meats and broths.

Plastic bags are quick, but they can tear, trap air, and aren't always truly airtight.

Glass containers on the other hand, are non-toxic, non-porous, reusable, and don't hold smells or stains. They're freezer- and oven-safe (minus the lid), and they give you a clear view of what's inside. No mystery blobs. Use mason jars, or clip-down lid containers.

Ideally, if using plastic, stick to food-grade, freezer-safe ones and rotate them out regularly.

Labelling:

- Include contents and date
- Optional: dog's name (if feeding multiples)

Label everything. Date it. Make it easy to grab and go.

Optional but helpful

If feeding homemade becomes your long-term plan, you might eventually invest in:

- A vacuum sealer (for freezing large batches)
- A (secondhand?) chest freezer (makes bulk preparation much easier)
- A food processor (if you're prepping for multiple dogs or dogs with chewing issues)
- A dehydrator
- A meat cleaver, for tougher meats and bones

But none of this is essential to get started. What matters is *consistency*, not equipment.

Action Step:
Take 10 minutes to do a pantry and fridge scan. Tick off what you already have from the list above, and circle three staples to pick up next time you shop. That's your base.

Common kitchen tools: L-R Strainer, cleaver, wooden spatula, masher, spoon strainer, pea strainer.

Buy in bulk and 'on special' to save

Chapter 8

Safe ingredients
(and what to avoid)

W hen you start feeding real food, it's natural to worry about what's safe. You're not alone. There's a lot of noise out there, some of it helpful, much of it exaggerated.

This chapter will give you a clear, level-headed breakdown of ingredients that are safe, helpful, and worth rotating into your dog's diet, and the few that truly *do* need to be avoided. Let's simplify it.

What about allergies?

Dog food allergies are most often caused by beef, chicken, dairy, wheat (and sometimes all grains). That doesn't mean these ingredients are bad across the board. It just means *if* your dog has chronic issues (itching, recurring ear infections, vomiting, or inconsistent stools), it may be worth trialling an exclusion period.

You'll find support for sensitive tummies and elimination diets in Part III.

Reminder for all meats:

- Choose human-grade, inspected meats whenever possible.

- Avoid heavily seasoned, smoked, or processed versions.

- Introduce exotic proteins slowly to watch for any sensitivities.

- Ensure proper storage and handling to prevent parasite transmission, especially with exotic or game meats.

The big "Yes" list

These foods are not only safe, but genuinely beneficial when included in the right amounts. See also Appendix D for additional choices.

Safe and Beneficial Foods for Dogs

Proteins (cooked or raw, depending on your feeding style):	Vegetables (lightly cooked or raw, chopped fine):
Chicken (meat, thighs, wings, necks) Beef (stew cuts, mince, heart, kidney) Turkey (lean and bony parts) Lamb and goat (including offcuts and organs) Pork (mince - unprocessed) Fish (sardines, mackerel, tinned salmon) Eggs (raw or scrambled, including shell for calcium) Exotic meats – see list.	Pumpkin Carrots Broccoli Zucchini Green beans Spinach (cooked or mixed in small amounts) Beetroot – Cook beetroot like pumpkin or potatoes (boiled/steamed) Capsicum (Bell peppers) – cooked or raw, remove seeds. Start small.
Carbs & Grains: Brown rice Pearl Barley Rolled oats Quinoa Sweet potato Pasta (plain, unsalted) Lentils and pulses Corn (in moderation)	**Fruits (in small amounts):** Apple (no seeds) Pears and apricots (remove stone first — highly dangerous if swallowed) Blueberries Banana Watermelon (no rind) and other melons
Healthy Fats: Olive oil Flaxseed (linseed) oil Coconut oil Fish oil Duck/Chicken fat (drained from broth or roasting pan)	**Extras & Boosters:** Bone broth (no onion or salt) Plain yoghurt (no sugar or xylitol) Apple cider vinegar (a few drops) Crushed eggshells (clean, dried, ground) Pumpkin puree – (canned or homemade) plain, unsweetened, and salt-free.

Grass-fed vs grain-fed meats?

Grass-fed usually contains more omega-3s, CLA (Conjugated linoleic acid) a type of polyunsaturated fatty acid, and antioxidants, better for inflammation and coat health.

Trust, but verify. You'll hear all sorts of advice online:

- "Dogs are carnivores. Don't feed them rice!"

- "Never give dogs fruit. It's sugar!"

- "Raw bones are dangerous!" / "Raw bones are essential!"

- Truth is, it depends; on your dog, on your method, and on your experience. This book will guide you toward cautious, thoughtful feeding, not dogmatic rules. (Pun intended).

Foods to use with care

These aren't dangerous, but they require moderation or a bit of knowledge before feeding.

- **Liver:** Incredibly nutrient-dense. Rich in vitamin A, iron, copper. Use once or twice a week, not daily.

- **Spinach, kale, and other oxalate-rich greens:** Too much may interfere with calcium absorption. Mix small amounts, rotate with other greens.

- **Raw bones:** Great for dental health *if* appropriate for your dog's size and chewing habits. Supervise always.

- **Dairy products:** Some dogs tolerate them well. Others don't. Start with small amounts, choose lactose-free milk, goat's milk, plain yoghurt or cottage cheese.

- **Tinned meats** (human food): Check for salt, preservatives, onion/garlic. Only use clean, plain options (e.g. sardines in water).

- **Corn:** In moderation. Use cooked, plain corn, (off the cob) or frozen. Avoid processed corn products. Some dogs digest it poorly.

A note on tomatoes – Caution

Ripe red tomatoes can be used in small amounts in cooked meals. They offer a good source of antioxidants, including lycopene. Avoid green tomatoes, leaves, and stems. These contain solanine, which is toxic.

You can substitute fresh tomato with plain, unsalted canned or puréed tomato as long as there are *no added onions, garlic, herbs, or spices.*

Look for ingredient labels that list only "tomatoes" or "tomatoes and water." Use no more than 1–2 tablespoons per meal for medium to large dogs. For small dogs, stick to teaspoons.

Tomato paste is too concentrated unless diluted first. A good rule is to mix 1 teaspoon paste with 2 tablespoons of water if using.

Tomato-based meals should be fed in moderation and not daily.

If a recipe calls for ¼ cup fresh chopped tomato, you can substitute:

- ¼ cup canned diced tomatoes, drained, OR 2–3 tbsp tomato purée, OR 2 tbsp diluted tomato paste (mix with a splash of water)

A note on mushrooms – Caution

Store-bought mushrooms like button, cremini, chaga, reishi and portobello are technically safe when cooked and fed in small amounts. Wild mushrooms are dangerous. Some are extremely toxic and hard to distinguish. Never feed if foraged outdoors. Safe if store-bought.

The no list (non-negotiables)

These are ingredients that should *never* be fed. No exceptions. (Each breed, each individual, tolerates them differently.)

- **Onion** (raw, cooked, powdered): Causes red blood cell damage. Hummus with garlic/onion

- **Garlic** (especially concentrated forms): The jury is out on this one. *High risk outweighs any benefit.* It is often used as a flea and tick preventative in small amounts.

- **Chocolate:** Toxic to the heart and nervous system.

- **Xylitol** (found in sugar-free gum, some yoghurts, icecream, peanut butter)**:** Causes liver failure, even in tiny doses.

- **Grapes and raisins:** Can cause kidney failure in some dogs, even one or two.

- **Cooked bones:** They splinter easily. Dangerous for choking and internal damage.

- **Avoid weight-bearing bones** of large animals (e.g. cow leg bones) as dogs can break their teeth.

- **Fat trimmings, ham (processed) bones, and fried food:** Can cause pancreatitis.

- **Mouldy or spoiled food:** Never risk "just a little." Dogs aren't garbage disposals.

- **Alcohol, caffeine, macadamia nuts, any nuts:** No, no, and no.

Exploring wild and exotic meats

In the diverse world of canine nutrition, incorporating a variety of protein sources can offer numerous benefits if you have access to them. Beyond the typical chicken, beef, and lamb, wild-caught and unconventional meats like game birds, rabbit, venison, kangaroo, pig, and goat, camel, horse, buffalo, bison and crocodile, present unique nutritional profiles that can enhance your dog's diet.

Advantages:

- Lean protein: Wild game meats are typically lower in fat and higher in protein compared to domesticated meats. For instance, venison and rabbit are known for their lean profiles, making them suitable for dogs requiring weight management.

- Rich in micronutrients: These meats often contain higher levels of essential nutrients like iron, zinc, and B vitamins, supporting overall health.

- Introducing different protein sources can prevent food sensitivities and allergies that may develop from prolonged exposure to a single protein.

- Are often cheaper than other meats, especially when buying in bulk.

Safety precautions:

- Freezing: It's recommended to freeze wild game meats for at least three weeks before feeding to eliminate potential parasites.

- Sourcing: Ensure meats are sourced from reputable suppliers or trusted hunters to avoid contamination. Beware of feeding if exotic diseases are present (for example, game birds, if bird flu is indicated).

Preparation tips:

- Cooking: While raw feeding is common, lightly cooking these meats can further reduce the risk of pathogens. Some are best cooked in the slow-cooker, because the meats are tougher, especially goat meat.

- Portioning: Due to their lean nature, you may need to adjust portion sizes to meet your dog's energy requirements.

Incorporating wild and unconventional meats into your dog's diet can provide nutritional diversity and address specific dietary needs. Always prioritize safety through proper sourcing and preparation, in accordance with veterinary advice.

Spotlight on specific meats

Bison: Very similar to buffalo but generally a bit richer in flavour. Bison meat provides excellent protein, zinc, and selenium. It's a great red meat option for rotating proteins in allergy management diets.

Buffalo (Water Buffalo): Buffalo is high in protein, low in fat, and an excellent source of omega-3 fatty acids compared to grain-fed beef. It's nutrient-dense and often hypoallergenic for sensitive dogs.

Camel: Camel meat is lean, rich in protein, and contains a good balance of iron and vitamin B. It can be a novel protein option for dogs with multiple food sensitivities, although availability may be difficult.

Crocodile: Lean, low-fat, and high in protein, crocodile meat is safe for dogs if properly sourced and cooked. It's considered a novel protein and can be useful for dogs with severe food intolerance. (Ensure it comes from a regulated supplier.)

Game Birds (Pigeon, Duck, Pheasant, Quail, Partridge):
Wild game birds are rich in protein, low in fat, and full of minerals like iron and phosphorus. They are ideal for variety, especially for smaller or medium-sized breeds who enjoy lighter meats. Always remove small bones before feeding.

Goat: Lean and nutrient-dense, goat meat provides a good balance of essential amino acids.

Horse Meat: High in protein, iron, and B vitamins, while relatively low in fat. It is often used in hypoallergenic diets, especially in Europe and parts of Asia. (Horse meat is frequently used in commercial dog foods for its ready availability.) If sourced ethically and inspected, horse meat can be a valuable alternative protein for dogs with food allergies or sensitivities.

Kangaroo: Exceptionally lean and high in B vitamins, kangaroo meat is a protein that can benefit dogs with allergies.

Pork (or Wild Boar): Offers a robust flavour and is a good source of monounsaturated fats, but should be fed in moderation due to higher fat content.

Rabbit: Highly digestible and low in fat, rabbit is an excellent choice for dogs with food sensitivities.

Venison: Rich in protein and iron, venison supports muscle development and oxygen transport in the blood.

Alternative fish sources

Fish can be a fantastic protein and omega-3 source, but the variety matters.

- **Tuna** (in moderation)**:** Dogs can eat cooked or tinned tuna (in spring water), but due to potential mercury levels, keep it occasional, especially for smaller dogs.

- **Trout:** Generally safe, particularly when cooked. Rich in omega-3s and easily digested. Avoid feeding raw freshwater fish in areas with salmon poisoning risk (e.g. Pacific Northwest USA).

- **Whitefish, mullet, snapper, perch, herring, cod, pilchards:** Great options. Low fat, digestible, and often well-tolerated by sensitive dogs.

- **Tinned salmon** (in water)**:** A good pantry staple with added calcium if bones are included. Choose options without added salt.

Avoid:

- Smoked fish (too salty)

- Breaded (crumbed) or battered fish

- Any fish with added spices, onion, or garlic

Turmeric Golden Paste For Dogs :

Considered by many to be a miracle paste for its anti-inflammatory properties, and certainly recommended. The pepper promotes greater absorption. Feed 1/2-1 teaspoon with meals, once daily.

Free image from a Pinterest Board

Ziggy, the whippet in quiet reflection.

Chapter 9

Meal prep tips for busy owners

L ife is full; kids, work, groceries, vet visits, muddy paw prints on clean floors. The idea of adding homemade dog food prep to all that? It can sound impossible.

But it's not.

This chapter is where we bring it all down to earth. Simple systems. Easy wins. A rhythm that works whether you're feeding one dog or five. You don't need to be perfectly organised. You just need a few good habits, and a freezer that's pulling its weight.

The golden rule: cook once, portion many

Just like meal prepping for yourself, feeding your dog well comes down to batching. Make food in bulk. Store it smart. And take the stress out of "what's for dinner?"

I will often cook the one meal when I have human-grade food, only adding in further ingredients for myself when I have spooned out doggy-dinner. If I cook rice for myself, I will cook a large batch for freezing and adding later to dog meals.

When you cook anything for your family, think ahead and make a larger batch which you can use for your dog. Although this may not always be your cheapest option (because you're using human grade), it certainly is a time saving option.

Step-by-step prep flow

- Choose your base recipe: Keep it simple: meat + carb + veg + oil. Pick ingredients you already have.

- Cook or combine ingredients: Use a big pot or slow-cooker. Add oils and supplements *after* cooking (to protect nutrients)

- Cool and portion: Use glass containers, freezer bags, or silicone trays. With smaller dogs, portion two meals in one. With larger dogs, cook double or triple amounts.
  Store enough in the fridge for 2–3 days, freeze the rest.

- Label and date: Include ingredients if feeding multiple dogs or doing elimination diets (or label with the dog's name).

- Defrost overnight in the fridge: Always serve room temperature, not cold straight from the fridge. When you take it out of the fridge, take the next one out of the freezer to defrost.

Time-savers for real life

- Use a slow-cooker overnight. Wake up to cooled food, ready to portion.

- Prep once a week. Sunday or your quietest evening works best.

- Keep "emergency" freezer packs for when life happens and dinner doesn't.

- Use leftovers. Plain rice, roast veggies, eggs. If it's dog-safe and unseasoned, use it.

- Create a basic menu rotation. Even 2–3 staple combinations will cover you for weeks.

- Stack the defrosting meals on a tray in your fridge. They sometimes leak, so this saves cleaning your fridge.

- When I take one meal out of the fridge, I take one out of the freezer to defrost for the next day.

- Buy specials in bulk. It is time-saving and cost effective.

You're not building a restaurant. You're building a rhythm.

Keep a running pantry list

Stick a notepad to the fridge. You'll know before the next prep day when you run out of:

- Oats

- Tinned sardines

- Frozen veggies

- Pumpkin

- Bone broth / cubes

You can even portion dry ingredients ahead of time, like jars of "dog dinner kits." Just add meat and cook.

Sample prep routine (for one medium dog)

Weekly Batch Cook:

- 1kg chicken thighs

- 3 cups cooked brown rice

- 2 cups steamed carrots + spinach (or cook from frozen)

- 2 tbsp olive oil

- 1 crushed eggshell

- 1 tbsp plain yoghurt (add fresh at serving)

Portion into 7–10 containers (depending on dog's weight). Label and freeze. All done in 90 minutes, for less than $20, no-panic meals all week. I do this alongside cooking my own meals.

Freezing considerations

Quality vs. Safety

Technically, homemade dog food, like any cooked human food, can stay safe in a freezer for several months (3–6 months is the broader food safety standard). Three weeks is a better guide. It isn't about it going *bad*, but about maintaining texture, taste, and nutrient quality:

- Freezer burn starts to affect moisture and palatability

- Fatty ingredients like fish or eggs degrade faster

- Some vitamins (like B-complex and E) slowly lose potency

And dogs *will* notice. Meals past that 3–4 week window tend to lose scent and taste appeal.

Rotation and freshness

Keeping the 3-week window:

- Encourages regular rotation, so meals don't sit and degrade

- Keeps your storage system simpler (what you see = what's fresh)

- Avoids freezer overload and forgotten containers from "that batch I made in July..."

Containers matter

Freezing in glass jars, vacuum-sealed bags, or airtight silicone trays will preserve food much longer than thin plastic containers or uncovered trays. Cover everything! So if you're well set up, your meals can easily go to 4–6 weeks or more with minimal quality loss.

For busy dog owners working from a fridge-top freezer, 3-4 weeks is the sweet spot. They're safe, fresh, and easy to manage. If you have a chest freezer, you can store much more. Yes, you can freeze longer. But 3 weeks keeps you in the zone of:

- Better flavour and scent for picky eaters

- Stronger nutrient retention

- Cleaner storage habits

If you're batch-prepping monthly? Just label clearly and rotate. You're still doing right by your dog.

Safe jar-freezing tips:

Use wide-mouth jars only. Regular jars with "shoulders" are more likely to crack. Wide-mouth jars allow for expansion.

Fill only ¾ full. Leave at least 2.5–3 cm (1 inch) of headspace at the top.

Cool fully in the fridge before freezing. Putting warm liquid straight into the freezer increases cracking risk.

Avoid sudden temperature change. Let jars chill gradually and freeze them upright.

Label clearly and freeze standing. Date and portion size are helpful, especially if you're storing multiple batches.

Alternatives to freezing in jars:

- Silicone muffin trays or ice cube trays (pop out and store in bags)

- Reusable freezer pouches or BPA-free ziplock bags

- Plastic deli containers (freezer-safe)

- Reuse yoghurt or ice cream tubs.

When you don't have time

Let's be honest. Some weeks, it all goes sideways. That's why this book supports mix-feeding and freezer backups.

Good options for "life happened" days:

- Tinned fish + rice + frozen veggies

- Scrambled eggs + oats + a spoon of yoghurt

- Leftover roast meat + sweet potato + bone broth cube

Ready-made essentials.

You may need to find these in specialist pet food shops, rather than the supermarket. Best options:

Bone broths Look for:

- labelled as dog-safe

- No onion, garlic, high sodium, or artificial flavouring

- Simple ingredients: bones, water, maybe turmeric or parsley

Do not use:

- "Flavoured" broths made for humans (usually too salty)

- Anything with "bouillon," "stock cubes," or "natural flavours" if unspecified. These usually have onion or garlic as flavorings.

Purees (pumpkin, sweet potato) Look for:

- labelled "100% Pure Pumpkin" or "100% Sweet Potato"

- No added sugar, salt, spices, or preservatives

Do not use:

- "Pumpkin Pie Filling" or "Spiced Pumpkin." Dangerous ingredients for dogs.

Collagen, fish oils, probiotics: Look for:

- Dog-specific formulas if possible

- Single-ingredient collagen powders (hydrolyzed preferred)

- Fish oils tested for purity (mercury-free certification if available)

- Probiotics with known strains (e.g., Lactobacillus, Bifidobacterium)

Do not use:

- Human collagen blends with flavourings

- Overdosing fat-based supplements (can cause diarrhoea)

Rotation and organisation

Rotate proteins every 1–2 weeks. Keep 1–2 days of food in the fridge, defrosting the rest gradually. Plan one "batch day" per week. Freeze 70%, refrigerate 30%. Always put *newest food at the back* to avoid forgetting older batches.

Reheating and serving

- Serve food at room temperature or slightly warm

- Do not microwave with supplements. Add those after warming

- Let frozen meals thaw in the fridge overnight

- Avoid serving cold straight from fridge. Some dogs resist, and it can be hard on digestion

Storage hygiene and safety

Wash containers and scoops regularly. Don't reuse bags unless they're washable. If it smells off, *it is*.

Don't use your own cutting boards. Reserve cutting boards for dogs only. Clean food bowls daily (yes, especially that slobbery one.)

Is it a perfect meal? Maybe not. But it's real. And it's better than rushing back to shelf kibble out of guilt.

You're not trying to be flawless. You're feeding with care.

Action Step:

Take inventory of your storage setup. Pick one prep day this week. Choose one recipe. Make enough for three meals.

Label two containers or bags with this week's date and contents. Try freezing one muffin tray of single serves. Cover the tray with aluminium foil.

That's. it. One step forward. You're already ahead of most. Future you will thank you.

Did you know?

I have written several books for horse lovers, and I write the Substack Newsletter, *Reflections on 50+ Years of Horse Breeding*.

Learn more here: https://jeanettegower.substack.com/

Also by Jeanette Gower

Available from Amazon, or the Author direct: https://books.by/jeanette-gower

Holly in full flight. Just look at her health and fitness!

Evie imitating a greyhound

Part II

Homemade Feeding Styles

"The Flying Nun" - Evie

Chapter 10

Raw feeding basics

A gentle start

R aw feeding for some, is a no-brainer. For others, it's intimidating. It comes with a reputation, either as a miracle diet or a risky fad.

As with most things, the truth sits in the middle.

Raw feeding can be incredibly beneficial *when done thoughtfully*. It's not about tossing your dog a hunk of meat and hoping for the best. It's about offering fresh, unprocessed food in a way that's digestible, safe, and nutritionally balanced. And of course you can mix raw with cooked.

This chapter introduces raw feeding in simple terms, what it is, who it suits, and how to begin. *I am convinced that it is the ultimate model for dog feeding*, but it doesn't suit all dogs, or households.

What is raw feeding?

Raw feeding means giving your dog food in its natural, uncooked state. That includes:

- Raw meat

- Raw meaty bones

- Organ meats

- Raw vegetables or fruit (optional)

- No grains, no fillers, no cooking

The idea is to mimic what dogs might have eaten before commercial food was invented.

But rather than guessing, we use what's known about canine nutrition to shape it responsibly.

Why consider raw?

Digestibility: Many dogs process raw meat more easily than cooked.
Skin and Coat: Improvements often seen within weeks.
Energy and Focus: Cleaner fuel = steadier temperament in some dogs.
Teeth: Raw bones are nature's toothbrush.
Poop: Smaller, firmer, and easier to pick up (really!).

Common myths (and the truth)

Some feeding models use a strict 80/10/10 ratio, that is, 80% muscle meat, 10% bone, 10% organ. The 80/10/10 ratio can also lead to excess calcium and vitamin A toxicity. While this is a common starting point in raw feeding, it doesn't take into account vegetables, seeds, broths, or fibre or omega-3s, if fed without adjustment. It also overlooks the needs of different ages, activity levels, or health concerns. This book uses a broader approach that adds plant foods, gentle cooking where needed, and more flexibility for real-life dogs and their real-life humans.

"Raw feeding is dangerous."
Raw feeding requires care, but done right, it's no riskier than raw meat in your own kitchen. Hygiene matters.

"Dogs need carbs."
Dogs are omnivores, but *not* carb-dependent. They thrive on protein and fat. Veg and small amounts of fruit provide fibre and micronutrients, not bulk energy.

"Raw diets are unbalanced."
Only if done on guesswork. A simple framework + variety = a strong foundation.

A gentle starting point

You don't need to go full "prey model" overnight. Start slow.

The slow-intro plan:

Week 1–2:
One raw meal a day, one cooked.
Soft meats like chicken, turkey, or lamb.
Avoid organ meats or bones at first.

Week 3:
Introduce soft raw bones (e.g. chicken necks, wings).
One small piece, always supervised.

Week 4+:
Begin rotating proteins.
Introduce organ meats once a week.
Optional: small amounts of blended veg or fruit.

What you'll need

- A basic scale (to portion by body weight)

- Access to fresh meat (supermarket is fine) but you'll usually find your local butcher or farmer's market can supply for you, often at farmgate prices, and better quality.

- Freezer space

- A calm plan (no rushing, no mixing raw + kibble at the same meal)

- Time to observe your dog closely in the first 2 weeks

Safety basics

Wash hands, surfaces, bowls. Keep cutting boards separate.
Don't leave raw food out longer than needed.
Defrost safely in the fridge. Use a tray to keep your fridge clean.
Don't feed cooked bones.
Store separately from human food when possible.

Sample balanced raw meal

For a 20kg / 44lbs dog (approx. 500g / 1lb2oz per day):

- 70% raw meaty parts (e.g. chicken thighs or lamb neck)

- 10% raw liver or kidney (once or twice a week)

- 10–15% blended veg (optional)

- Small drizzle of flaxseed or fish oil

Remember: balance happens over *time*, not every bowl.

When raw might not be ideal

- Dogs with compromised immune systems

Salmon frames from the fish market. Buy a frozen 2kg box and feed every now and then. Large dogs love them.

- Dogs recovering from illness or surgery

- Owners uncomfortable with raw meat prep

- Households with young children or immuno-compromised members (due to handling risks)

If any of these apply, cooked or hybrid feeding may be a better fit. There's no one-size-fits-all.

Feeding bones

Bones can be a fantastic addition to your dog's diet, offering nutritional benefits, dental health support, and mental stimulation. However, it's crucial to approach bone feeding with knowledge and care to ensure your dog's safety and well-being.

Nutritional benefits:

- Calcium and Phosphorus: Essential minerals for strong bones and teeth.

- Marrow: Rich in fat and nutrients, beneficial for energy and overall health.

Dental health: Chewing on raw bones can help reduce plaque and tartar buildup, promoting healthier gums and teeth.

Mental stimulation:

- Gnawing on bones satisfies your dog's natural chewing instincts, providing mental enrichment and reducing boredom.

- Very useful when dogs are teething.

The do's of bone feeding

Choose raw bones: Always opt for raw bones, as cooking can make bones brittle and prone to splintering, posing serious health risks.

- Select appropriate sizes: Small dogs: Chicken wings, necks, feet or drumsticks, medium to large dogs: Lamb ribs, beef knuckles, or turkey necks or feet.

- Supervise chewing: Always monitor your dog while they're chewing to prevent choking or ingestion of large bone fragments.

- Introduce gradually: Start with small amounts to allow your dog's digestive system to adjust.

- Store properly: Keep raw bones frozen until use, and thaw in the refrigerator to maintain freshness and prevent bacterial growth.

The don'ts of bone feeding

- Avoid cooked bones: Cooking alters the structure of bones, making them brittle and dangerous.

- Steer clear of weight-bearing bones: Bones like beef femurs are extremely hard and can break your dog's teeth. Ask your butcher to slice them length-ways, so they can access the spongy inside.

- Don't feed small bones to large dogs: Small bones can be swallowed whole, leading to choking or intestinal blockages.

- Avoid bones with sharp edges: Splintered bones can cause internal injuries.

- Don't leave bones unattended: Discard bones after a reasonable chewing period to prevent spoilage or over-consumption.

Tips for safe bone feeding

- Frequency: Offer bones 1-2 times per week as a treat or supplement, not as a meal replacement.

- Observe stool quality: White, crumbly stools may indicate too much bone intake; adjust accordingly.

- Before introducing bones, especially if your dog has existing health issues, seek professional advice.

Summary

Feeding bones can be a rewarding experience for both you and your dog when done correctly. By choosing the right types of bones, supervising sessions, and following safety guidelines, you can enhance your dog's diet and overall well-being.

> Action Step:
>
> Try replacing one meal this week with raw mince, finely grated carrot, and a spoon of plain yoghurt. Watch your dog's reaction. Track stool, energy, coat. You're not "raw feeding yet." You're simply exploring.

Holly and Misty love raw meaty shanks as a treat.

Chapter 11

Cooked meals

Stovetop and slow-cooker options

For many owners, cooked food feels like the natural place to begin. It's familiar. Picky eaters (like Evie) won't eat raw. Cooked meals seem safe. And it smells like dinner, because it is.

Cooked meals are gentle on the gut, easy to prepare in batches, and often more accepted by picky dogs or those transitioning off processed food. This chapter will walk you through how to build balanced, cooked meals using simple methods: stove-top or slow-cooker.

You don't need recipes just yet. You need structure to familiarize you with the basics.

Why cooked meals work

Cooking helps:

- Break down starches in grains and vegetables

- Reduce bacteria risk (especially for beginners or immune-compromised dogs)

- Make harder cuts of meat more digestible

- Ease transitions for dogs with sensitive stomachs

Plus, it suits busy households. You can prepare one pot, portion it out, and not think about it again for a week.

Method 1: stove-top

This is your classic pot of stew. Simple, flexible, and easy to scale.

Basic formula:

- 50–70% protein (chicken, beef, lamb, fish)

- 15–25% carbohydrates (rice, oats, sweet potato)

- 10–20% vegetables (carrots, pumpkin, green beans)

- Optional: herbs, oils, supplements added at the end

Simmer ingredients until cooked through. Cool fully before adding oils or boosters. Then portion and store.

Cooked Meal Staples

Proteins:	Vegetables:
Chicken (mince, thighs, frames) Beef (mince, stewing cuts) Turkey (neck, mince) Lamb (offcuts, hearts) Sardines or tinned fish (added after cooking) Eggs (boiled or scrambled separately)	Carrots, Green beans, Broccoli, Zucchini Leafy greens in small amounts (spinach, kale) Pumpkin / butternut
Carbs & Grains:	**Extras:** (after cooking):
Brown or white rice Rolled oats Sweet potato or pumpkin Barley or couscous	Olive or flaxseed oil Ground eggshell Yoghurt or kefir Turmeric paste Bone broth cubes

Method 2: slow-cooker

This is the weeknight hero. Set it up in the morning, come home to cooked meals ready to pack.

Best for:

- Dogs who need soft food

- Owners feeding multiple dogs

- Using tougher meat cuts that benefit from slow-cooking (such as goat).

Tips:

- Cut all ingredients to similar sizes for even cooking

- Add water or broth to prevent drying out

- Cook on low for 6–8 hours

- Stir before portioning to evenly distribute ingredients

Storage and rotation

Cooked meals can be:

- Stored in fridge: up to 3 days

- Stored in freezer: up to 4 weeks

- Rotated every 2–3 weeks to prevent nutrient gaps

Portion sizes will depend on weight and activity level, but for a 20kg / 44lbs dog, plan on ~500g / 1lb2oz per day, split across two meals.

Trouble-shooting cooked feeding

- Dog won't eat it? Try warming it slightly. Mix in a spoon of bone broth or tinned sardines.

- Too runny? Add oats or mashed vegetables to thicken the base.

- Dry coat? Increase healthy fats: olive oil, sardines, egg yolk.

- Pull back on fat, simplify the ingredients, and go blander for a few days.

When cooked food is ideal

- For dogs recovering from illness

- For owners nervous about raw feeding

- For dogs with dental issues or chewing challenges

- For dogs with sensitive guts or allergies

- For households already cooking meals, it's an easy extension

---

Action Step:

Choose one day this week to try a stove-top or slow-cooker meal. Use the ingredient list from Chapter 8 and build one batch. It doesn't have to be perfect. It just has to be yours.

Slow-cooked beef chunks with pumpkin and green beans. Freeze any juices and use later.

Chapter 12

Roasting

Flavourful options your dog will love

R oasting meats and vegetables is a safe and flavourful way to add variety to your dog's meals, and many dogs enjoy the texture and aroma of roasted food.

Why roast?

- Enhanced flavour without added seasoning

- Natural caramelisation brings out sweetness in veggies like pumpkin, carrots, and sweet potato

- Fat can be drained off easily from roasted meat, making it leaner

- Great for batch cooking and mixing with softer foods like stews or purees

- No need to stand over the cooking. Just set the timer and forget.

Roasting guidelines

Meats:

- Roast plain, without seasoning, onion, garlic, or marinades

- Use lean cuts: lamb shoulder, beef chuck, chicken thighs (skinless), turkey necks or meat offcuts.

- Roast at 160–180°C (325–350°F) until cooked through. (An electric frypan can be an excellent choice for roasting.)

- Drain excess fat and chop or shred before serving

- Great for dogs who enjoy chewing on chunks

Veggies:

- Cube or slice pumpkin, sweet potato, zucchini, parsnip, carrot, or beet-root.

Note: dogs can eat soft, roasted pumpkin skin. No need to remove the skin for roasting. If unsure, just spoon out the soft flesh after cooking. If the skin is too tough, it might pose a choking risk.

- Toss lightly in olive oil or coconut oil

- Roast at 180°C (350°F) for 30–40 minutes or until soft

- Avoid hard, raw chunks for small dogs. Mash or blend if needed

What to avoid

- No onions, garlic, or shallots

- No added salt or spice rubs

- Avoid blackened or over-roasted edges (these can be hard to digest)

- Don't use tinned gravies or sauces

- Avoid stringy meats/vegetables *if* the dog has digestive issues or tends to gulp large chunks

- Remove cooked bones

Roasting is also an excellent way to use up slightly tired vegetables from the fridge. Let them cool, chop or mash, and mix into your dog's regular meals.

This small change gives your dog a new texture, fresh smell, and keeps you inspired to keep feeding well, with confidence.

Action Step:

This week, try roasting one meal for your dog instead of boiling or stewing. Choose a lean meat (like lamb, chicken or fish) and pair it with two dog-safe vegetables such as pumpkin, sweet potato, or zucchini.

Chapter 13

Soft cooked meals

Gently cooked, blended meals

S ome dogs need their food a little softer. Whether it's dental trouble, recovery from illness, or just sensitive digestion, there are times when gently cooked or blended meals make all the difference.

These meals are simple, nourishing, and ideal for easing the transition into homemade feeding, especially for senior dogs, small breeds, or any dog who picks around chunky food like a suspicious toddler.

Let's break down when and why to use this style, and how to build meals that are easy on the gut but still rich in everything your dog needs.

What are gently cooked or blended meals?

- Gently cooked: Lightly simmered or steamed ingredients, often chopped or mashed

- Blended: Fully cooked ingredients pureed into a soft, spoonable mix. Think "dog stew" or a warm mash

You're not sacrificing nutrition. You're just making it more accessible.

Who benefits most?

Senior dogs: Less chewing, easier digestion
Toothless or dental-sensitive dogs: No more avoiding chunky kibble
Post-surgery dogs: Soothing, soft meals support recovery
Picky eaters: Warmer, smellier blends often appeal more
Rescues: Stressed stomachs need soft starts

The benefits of soft food

- Easier on the stomach

- Faster nutrient absorption

- Better hydration (especially if feeding broth-based meals)

- Less chewing effort

- Less risk of choking for small or anxious eaters

And for the owner? It's fast. You can prep a 1-2 week's worth in one pot.

What to include

Use the same core formula as with standard cooked meals; just prepare it differently.

Soft Food Staples

Proteins:	Vegetables:
Chicken or turkey mince Boiled eggs Sardines or white fish Lamb mince or slow-cooked stew meat	Steamed and mashed carrots, zucchini, pumpkin Finely chopped spinach or broccoli Blend until smooth or lightly mashed
Carbs & Grains: Well-cooked brown rice Mashed sweet potato Porridge oats (softened) Cooked Barley	**Extras:** Bone broth Olive or flaxseed (linseed) oil Probiotic Greek yoghurt Ground eggshell or calcium supplement Avoid anything hard to puree – like raw kale, bone or fatty gristle.

Prep tips

- Cook everything thoroughly, including meats and veg

- Use a stick blender or food processor for texture control

- Portion into small tubs or trays for easy thawing

- Serve slightly warm (never hot). Smell matters to dogs

Ideal texture

Think:

- Spoonable, not runny

- Smooth with some soft texture

- No large chunks or hard-to-chew bits

This consistency helps prevent gulping and promotes easy digestion, especially in dogs who eat quickly or who've lost teeth.

How long to feed this way?

You can feed soft meals short-term (e.g. after surgery) or long-term, especially for elderly dogs or those with chronic dental or gut conditions.

There's no downside. Just keep variety up and ensure you're still meeting all nutrient needs.

Sample gently cooked meal (blended)

- 1 cup cooked chicken mince

- ½ cup cooked brown rice

- ¼ cup steamed pumpkin + carrot

- 1 tsp olive oil

- 1 tbsp bone broth

- Pinch of ground eggshell or vet-approved calcium

Blend into a soft, warm mash. Serve and watch tails wag.

Action Step:

Try preparing one blended meal this week. Note your dog's response; how quickly they eat, stool consistency, and general energy. For older dogs, it can be a turning point.

Soft-cooked meals are ideal for senior dogs.

Chapter 14

Mix-feeding

Combining homemade with store-bought

N ot everyone can cook every meal from scratch. And not every dog thrives on an all-homemade diet. The good news? You don't have to choose one or the other.

Mix-feeding, blending homemade meals with commercial options, is a flexible, realistic approach that can still dramatically improve your dog's nutrition without sacrificing convenience.

This chapter shows how to do it well, without undermining the benefits of either.

What is mix-feeding?

Mix-feeding means feeding:

- Some homemade meals (cooked, raw, or blended)

- Some commercial dog food (kibble, loaf or canned)

You might feed:

- Kibble in the morning, homemade at night

- Homemade meals on weekends, kibble during the week

- Commercial base meals topped with homemade additions ("toppers")

It's all about flexibility. The goal is to *elevate* your dog's nutrition, not overhaul it overnight.

Why choose mix-feeding?

- Time Management: Homemade doesn't need to be all-or-nothing

- Budget-Friendly: Stretch premium ingredients further

- Easy Transition: Gently ease into a new feeding style

- Digestive Support: Add moisture, fibre, and fresh nutrients to dry food

- Customisation: Tailor meals without tossing out your existing food routine

How to mix without upsetting your dog's gut

Dogs do best with predictability, especially in their digestion. So if you're switching between meal types, keep it structured.

Example routine:

- Morning: Dry or canned commercial food

- Evening: Home-cooked or raw bowl

- Add consistent elements to both (e.g. same oils, same fibre source)

Or:

- Mon–Fri: Kibble

- Sat–Sun: Fresh meals, cooked or raw

- Midweek: Toppers like sardines or egg on kibble

The key is rhythm. Avoid random mixing. Your dog's body likes a routine.

Safe homemade toppers (daily or occasional)

Adding real food to kibble is an easy way to boost nutrition, even if you're not ready to go full homemade.

Here are simple, safe additions:

- A spoonful of cooked pumpkin or sweet potato

- A raw or boiled egg

- A splash of bone broth or goat's milk

- A sprinkle of sardines or tinned mackerel

- A spoon of plain yoghurt or kefir

- A handful of steamed green beans

- A drizzle of olive oil or flaxseed oil

All of these improve hydration, add fresh enzymes or fats, and boost flavour. You'll likely notice your dog's enthusiasm shift immediately.

Watch for portion creep

One risk with mix-feeding is overfeeding. Dogs love fresh food, and will often try to convince you they need more.

To avoid weight gain:

- Reduce the amount of kibble proportionally when adding fresh food. Don't leave kibble out for "free choice."

- Weigh meals for a while until you get used to the new balance

- Adjust slowly. Watch stool consistency and energy levels

A general guide:

- 25% fresh food + 75% kibble is a safe starting point

- Build up to 50/50 if your dog tolerates it well, e.g. kibble in the morning, homemade at night.

When mix-feeding might not work

There are times when dogs don't do well switching between meal types.

Caution if:

- Your dog has chronic pancreatitis or a highly sensitive gut

- You're feeding raw and kibble in the same bowl (not always ideal)

- Your dog eats too fast, risking bloat when mixing styles

In these cases, consistent feeding (either fully homemade or a vet-advised commercial plan) may be better.

Action Step:

Pick one meal this week to "upgrade" with a fresh food topper. Start simple, an egg, a spoon of pumpkin, a splash of broth. See how your dog responds. Small steps = real gains.

Omelette with zucchini and sardines topper

Part III

Life Stages and Special Diets

Jumping for sheer joy of life

Chapter 15

Pregnant and nursing bitches

And their newborn pups.

P regnancy and nursing are demanding stages for a dog's body. She's not just eating for two. She may be eating for eight. And yet, overfeeding the wrong things can cause more harm than help.

This chapter walks you through what a pregnant or lactating dog actually needs, how her requirements shift over time, and how to build meals that nourish her *without* overloading her.

Feeding through pregnancy: a timeline

A typical canine pregnancy lasts about 63 days. Her nutritional needs evolve through each stage:

Weeks 1–4:

No major increase in food needed
Stick to her usual, balanced meals
Focus on quality over quantity

Tip: Early weight gain can lead to oversized pups and whelping difficulty.

Weeks 5–7:

Increase intake gradually (by 10–25%)
Add more fat and protein
Shift to 3 meals/day to ease stomach compression

Begin adding DHA (brain development for pups).

Week 8–9:

Increase meals to 3–4 per day
Appetite may decrease. Offer smaller, more frequent meals
Focus on soft, easy-to-digest food
Avoid heavy bones or rich organs at this stage

What is DHA (and why it matters for nursing moms)?

DHA stands for Docosahexaenoic Acid.
It's a type of omega-3 fatty acid that plays a crucial role in brain, eye, and nervous system development, not just in humans, but in dogs too.

Why it's important for nursing moms:

- Puppies get their early brain-building nutrients from their mother's milk.

- DHA helps develop strong vision, sharper learning ability, better memory, and calmer behaviour later on.

- Without enough DHA, puppies might have delayed neural development or weaker immune systems.

Where dogs get DHA naturally:

- Sardines, mackerel, anchovies (small oily fish)

- Salmon oil, krill oil

- Green-lipped mussel supplements

- Egg yolk (to a smaller degree)

- Some high-quality meats (wild or grass-fed) contain small amounts

Why add DHA to the mom's diet:

- Boosts milk quality

- Supports the puppies' growing brains and eyes *before and after* birth

- Helps the mom's own joints, skin, and immunity while her body recovers

Simple way to include DHA in homemade dog food:

- Add a small amount of fish oil (sardine, salmon, or krill) 2–3 times a week to meals during pregnancy and nursing.

- Use fresh sardines or tinned sardines in water (no salt or additives).

Important: Always introduce DHA-rich foods gradually to avoid upset tummies.

Calcium supplementation

Calcium deficiency can lead to eclampsia (muscle tremors, seizures). Start calcium-rich foods and continue through nursing. Use natural sources like bone broth, eggshell powder. Calcium timing in pregnant and nursing dogs is one of the most commonly misunderstood issues in canine nutrition.

Here's the clear breakdown, based on best-practice veterinary guidance:

The short version:

- Do NOT supplement calcium during most of pregnancy. (Check with your vet if unsure).

- Do supplement calcium once the puppies are born and nursing begins.

Why not supplement during pregnancy?

Giving extra calcium during pregnancy can disrupt the mother's natural hormonal regulation of calcium. Her body becomes "lazy" about mobilising calcium from bones, and when sudden demands hit during nursing, she can't keep up.

This can lead to a dangerous condition after birth called **eclampsia** (low blood calcium), causing:

- Muscle tremors

- Panting

- Seizures

- In severe cases, death

So paradoxically, supplementing too early makes calcium deficiency more likely after whelping.

What to avoid

- Overfeeding in early pregnancy.

- Organ meats in excess (especially liver, too much vitamin A).

- Raw bones during late pregnancy or nursing (risk of GI upset).

- Foods with strong smells or flavours (can put her off food).

- Poor hydration, can affect milk production.

Monitor body condition closely

During pregnancy:

- Weight should increase gradually from week 4

- Keep an eye on energy, coat, and stool

- No weight gain in early weeks = good

- Steady weight gain in final weeks = expected

During nursing:

- Weight may drop initially

- Appetite will be high. Don't restrict unless advised by a vet

- Check teats and nipples for inflammation or infection signs

When should calcium be increased?

Start feeding natural calcium-rich foods (bone broth, sardines, eggshell powder) immediately after birth **or** use a commercial supplement as advised by your vet, when milk production ramps up. Some breeds which have large litters are particularly prone to eclampsia.

This helps meet her increased calcium needs without interfering with her body's natural calcium-release mechanisms during pregnancy.

Feeding during nursing

This is the most calorie-demanding stage of her life. Some working dogs will even want to continue working though they have puppies to raise. Close them in a quiet space away from their working neighbours to reduce excitement. Feed 3–4 meals daily or allow supervised free-feeding and ensure continual access to clean water.

Double (or even triple) her normal food intake.
Keep meals high-fat, high-protein, and hydrating.
Give easy to digest foods.

A lactating dog feeding 6–8 pups may need:

- 3–5% of her body weight in food per day, depending on breed

- Energy-dense meals: meat, bone broth, egg yolk, fish, high-quality carbs

---

Ideal ingredients

- Soft-cooked meats (chicken, lamb, turkey, beef mince)

- Bone broth for hydration and minerals

- Eggs (raw or cooked) for protein and fat

- Sardines or fish oil for omega-3s and DHA

- Pumpkin or sweet potato for easy calories

- Yogurt or kefir for calcium and gut support

- Leafy greens in small amounts for iron and folate

Action Step:

If your dog is pregnant or nursing, adjust one meal this week to boost soft protein and hydration. Think scrambled egg with broth over rice. Watch for improved energy and appetite.

Please note: there is a "What to have on hand for whelping" guide, in the Appendix.

Nutrient dense food, ideal for nursing mums.

Chapter 16

Newborn puppies

Hand raising and topping up

R aising young puppies without their mother is possible, but it takes care, planning, and the right milk. While homemade formulas can help in emergencies, a proper vet-approved puppy milk powder is safer and more reliable for long-term feeding.

- For hand-rearing whole litters under 4–5 weeks, a commercially formulated vet-approved puppy milk powder is *far better* and *time saving*.

- **Why?**
  Commercial formulas (like Esbilac, Divetelact, or Royal Canin Puppy Milk) are specifically balanced for puppies; protein, fat, calcium, DHA, and much safer long-term than homemade milk, which can be unbalanced.

Homemade puppy milk formula (Under 5 weeks old)

This formula is designed to mimic mother's milk, rich in fat, protein, and easily digestible sugars, but gentle enough for tiny, developing tummies. These formulas are provided for emergency or short term use.

Main orphan puppy formula

- 240ml (1 cup) whole goat's milk (or goat milk powder made up as directed)

- 1 raw egg yolk (from a fresh, clean egg)

- 1 tablespoon plain full-fat yoghurt (unsweetened, no flavourings)

- 1 teaspoon corn syrup (light) or honey (only if puppy is strong, optional)

- 1 drop infant probiotic (optional but very helpful for gut support)

How to prepare:

- Blend all ingredients gently (don't froth too much, just combine).

- Warm to body temperature before feeding (about 37°C / 98°F – *feels warm but not hot* on your wrist).

- Store unused formula in fridge for up to **24 hours**. Always re-warm individual feeds.

Feeding notes:

- Feed every 2–3 hours (including overnight) until 3 weeks old.

- By 3–4 weeks, start reducing night feeds and begin introducing mushy foods.

- Use a proper sterile puppy bottle or syringe (small amounts at a time to prevent aspiration).

Emergency/alternative formula (if goat's milk is not available)

- 240ml (1 cup) full-fat lactose-free cow's milk (or evaporated milk diluted 1:1 with water)

- 1 raw egg yolk

- 1 tablespoon full-fat plain yoghurt

- 1 teaspoon corn syrup or small amount of honey

(*Note:* Goat's milk is ideal because it's naturally easier to digest. Cow's milk *alternatives* are fine short-term but can cause a little more gas.)

Important milk safety reminders:

- Never use straight cow's milk. Too much lactose = diarrhoea risk.

- No plant milks (almond, soy, oat). Not appropriate for puppies.

- Do not add raw egg white, only yolk! (Egg white alone can block biotin absorption.)

- Always test bottle flow, drops, not streams, to prevent choking.

- Burp pups after each feed (gently like a human baby.) Hold upright and pat back softly.

- Stimulate toileting with a warm, damp cloth if under 3 weeks old.

Golden rule:

Warmth before food. A chilled puppy cannot digest milk properly. Always warm gently first if the pup feels cool.

Puppy Feeding Amount Guidelines

Puppy Age	Amount per Feed (ml / tsp / oz)	Frequency
0–1 week	2–4 ml (½–¾ tsp)	Every 2 hours
1–2 weeks	5–8 ml (1–1¾ tsp)	Every 3 hours
2–3 weeks	8–10 ml (1¾–2 tsp)	Every 3–4 hours
3–4 weeks	10–15 ml (2–3 tsp / ⅓–½ oz)	Every 4 hours + start soft food
4–5 weeks	Transition to slurry/mash	4 times daily

Handy References:

- 5 ml = 1 teaspoon (tsp)
- 30 ml = 1 fluid ounce (oz)

Emergency backups

- Ready-to-mix emergency puppy milk powder (vet-approved brand)

- Electrolyte solution (puppy-safe, for dehydration risks)

- Vet phone number on standby (know your after-hours options)

Don't you just want to snuggle them?

How to adjust feeding for different sized or breed puppies

Not all puppies are created equal, and that's a beautiful thing. Tiny breeds, giant breeds, and everything in between grow at different speeds and need tailored feeding to support healthy development without overloading their little systems. Here's how to think about it simply:

Toy and small breeds (under 5kg / 11lb adult weight)

Tend to burn calories faster (higher metabolism).
Need slightly smaller, more frequent feeds to avoid blood sugar crashes.
May only take 2–5 ml per feed in the first week. They have very tiny stomachs!

Tip: Tiny breeds benefit from more feeds spaced evenly. Every 2–2.5 hours at first.

Medium breeds (10–25kg / 22–55lb adult weight)

Follow the standard feeding charts fairly closely.
Gradual increases based on appetite, body condition, and weight checks.
Monitor for steady, not rapid, weight gain (about 5–10% body weight daily at first).

Tip: Don't force large volumes if puppy is slow. Small, regular feeds are safer.

Large breeds (30kg+ / 66lb+ adult weight)

Grow fast, but bones need time to strengthen.
Often eat bigger amounts earlier than small breeds.
Be careful not to overfeed, too rapid growth can damage joints.

Tip: Increase feed volume by 10–20% above normal charts if weight gain is slow. Focus on consistent calories, but don't push to "chubby" just because they're big!

How to check if you're feeding enough (without scales)

- Puppy should have a full but not tight belly after feeding

- Should settle calmly to sleep after feeds

- Good urine output (pale yellow, not dark)

- Steady daily weight gain (no big drops)

If in doubt, slightly smaller, more frequent feeds are safer than pushing large meals. If the puppy cries constantly after a feed, check for air bubbles (burp!) before assuming hunger.

Quick Adjustment Guide

Puppy Type	Feeding Adjustment
Tiny Toy Breeds	-10% feed volume per meal, add extra feed
Medium Breeds	Standard charts
Large/Giant Breeds	+10–20% feed volume if slow gain

In a nutshell:

Tiny pups = tiny but frequent meals. Big pups = balanced, steady feeding without overloading joints.

Understanding puppy growth curves

Puppy growth isn't a straight line. It's a gentle wave of rapid early gains, followed by slower, steadier progress as they mature. Knowing what healthy growth looks like can help you spot problems early, without needing to overthink every meal. Here's a simple way to visualise it:

Normal puppy growth curve:

- 0–2 weeks:
  Steady, daily weight gain (5–10% of birth weight per day). Puppies double birth weight by ~10 days old.

- 2–4 weeks:
  Continued rapid growth, beginning stronger movements and first play behaviours. Still heavily reliant on milk.

- 4–6 weeks:
  Starts weaning onto mushy solids. Growth slows a little, but energy increases!

- 6–12 weeks:
  Fast growth again as skeletal and muscular systems develop. Pups are usually triple to quadruple their birth weight by now.

- 3–6 months:
  Rapid growth phases, especially in medium to large breeds. Appetite may spike during growth spurts.

- 6–12 months:
  Slowing to mature size. Smaller breeds finish growing sooner (~9–12 months); giant breeds may grow until 18–24 months.

Signs of unhealthy growth

Too rapid growth:

- Puppy looks "roly-poly" or heavy too early

- Pacing, joint stiffness, poor coordination

- Risk of joint stress (especially large breeds)

Too slow growth:

- Ribs or spine very visible

- Weak suckling, lethargy

- Low weight gain (less than 5% per day in newborns)

Golden growth rules

- Steady, not extreme. Expect gentle upward weight trends

- Adjust feeding slightly every few days based on the body, not just the scale

- Support bones, not just bellies. Don't push heavy calories too fast

Simple home check:

- Feel ribs easily, but they shouldn't be sticking out

- Puppy should have a "full but soft" belly after feeds

- Active, alert between naps

To Action: Weaning
Around 3–4 weeks of age, puppies will begin tasting soft food. Reduce the mother's food slightly once pups are consistently eating on their own (around 6–7 weeks). Gradually introduce: soft-cooked meats, blended veg and rice, bone broth.

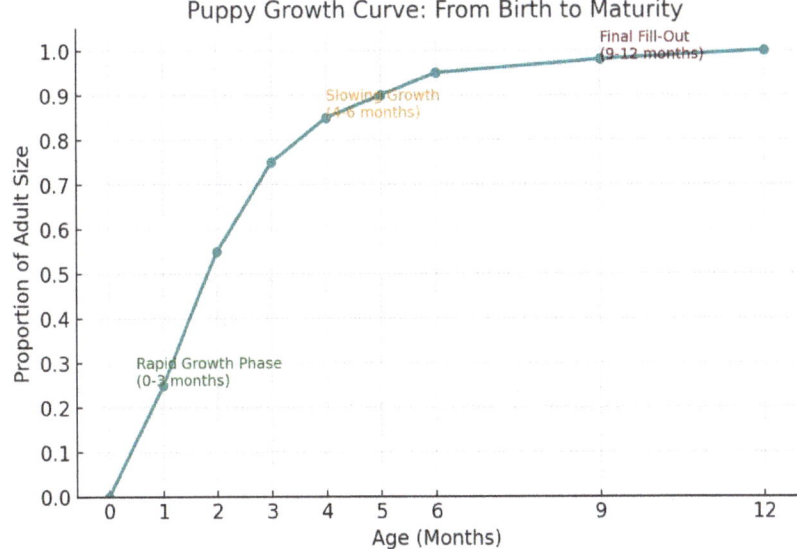

Lively Tenterfield puppies having a play.

Chapter 17

Growing puppies

Nutrition for growth

P uppies aren't just smaller dogs. They're dogs in fast-forward. Every week brings growth in size, strength, learning, and play. That kind of development doesn't happen without fuel. But it's not just about *more* food. It's about the *right* kind of food, given at the right time, in the right way.

What puppies need (that adults don't)

Growing bodies have higher demands:

- More protein, for tissue growth and immune development

- More fat, for energy and brain function

- More calcium and phosphorus, for bone growth

- Smaller, more frequent meals, because little tummies can't hold much at once

- Gentle digestibility, less tolerance for "rich" or spicy foods

The aim is to grow slowly and steadily, not just fast.

Puppy feeding schedule by age

Here's a simple breakdown:

8–12 weeks:
4 small meals/day
Mostly soft or blended textures. Use a masher or food blender.

3–6 months:
3 meals/day
Introduce more solid foods, gentle bones if appropriate

6–12 months:
2 meals/day
Larger portions, wider variety, begin shifting toward adult maintenance

Tip: Large breed puppies may benefit from remaining on a "puppy-style" diet (higher fat/protein) until 12–18 months, to support joint and skeletal development without rapid weight gain.

Key nutrients for puppies

Protein:
Essential for muscle growth, immune strength, and repair.
Use soft meats like chicken, turkey, beef mince, and tinned fish.

Fat:
Supports energy needs and cognitive development.
Include oily fish, egg yolk, or small amounts of olive/fish oil.

Calcium + phosphorus:
Crucial for skeletal health.
Ground eggshell, small raw meaty bones, or vet-approved calcium source.

DHA (an omega-3):
Supports brain development.
Found in sardines, salmon, and fish oils.

Avoiding common pitfalls

- Too much calcium from bone. Can interfere with joint development

- Switching foods too quickly. Can cause diarrhoea and poor absorption

- Overfeeding, leads to rapid growth, which increases risk of orthopedic issues

- Underfeeding, stunts development and weakens the immune system

Tip: Always monitor weight, coat, energy, and stool, not just the empty bowl.

Homemade meals for puppies

What to keep in mind

Portion based on 5–10% of body weight per day, depending on age and size. Feed frequently. Puppies burn through calories fast. Watch stool consistency as your biggest sign of how food is settling. Rotate proteins slowly to avoid overload

Sample meal for a 10kg puppy (~500–800g/day split into 3 meals):

- 60% soft-cooked chicken

- 20% mashed sweet potato or rice

- 15% blended veg (zucchini, spinach, carrot). Use a blender.

- 1 tsp sardine oil or egg yolk

- Pinch of crushed eggshells

Treats and training

Puppies learn with food. Use small pieces of their regular meals as training rewards. If adding store-bought treats, choose:

- Low-ingredient, meat-based

- No colours, sugars, preservatives

- No milk bones or commercial biscuits during the sensitive early stage

You'll find a full treat section in Part VI.

Quick body check

Here's a simple visual reference:

- Too thin? Ribs clearly visible, spine prominent

- Just right? Can feel ribs with light pressure, waist visible from above

- Too heavy? Can't feel ribs, no waist, rounded belly

Teeth and the chew phase

If your pup is still in the puppy teeth stage (roughly 3 weeks to 6 months old), chances are they're chewing everything they shouldn't: shoes, chair legs, remote controls, you name it.

That's not misbehaviour. It's instinct. Just like toddlers teething, puppies chew to:

- Relieve discomfort as baby teeth fall out

- Explore textures with their mouths

- Loosen gums and encourage healthy adult tooth development

You can redirect destructive chewing and support dental development by offering safe, age-appropriate bones and chews.

Helpful options:

- Frozen carrot sticks (soothe gums)

- Soft raw bones like chicken necks or wings

- Dehydrated tendons or strips (single-ingredient, digestible)

- Frozen yoghurt and banana cubes

Not only do these options reduce furniture damage, but they also lay a positive foundation for lifelong chewing behaviour, and support cleaner teeth during a crucial stage of dental transition.

Vet check-ins

- Weigh regularly, especially for medium/large breeds

- Monitor teeth and joint development

- Discuss vaccines, worming, and flea schedules

- Discuss micro-chipping, desexing and other specifics, like hernia.

- Ask about breed-specific concerns (e.g. hip issues in Labradors, back issues in Dachshunds)

- Discuss DNA testing for genetic diseases and colours.

Your feeding plan should evolve as your pup grows. Keep checking in, with your dog, and your vet.

Puppy Feeding Guide by Weight

Puppy Weight (kg / lb)	Daily Food Amount (g / oz)
2 kg (4.4 lb)	100–160g (3.5–5.6 oz)
5 kg (11 lb)	250–400g (8.8–14 oz)
10 kg (22 lb)	500–800g (17.6–28 oz)
15 kg (33 lb)	750–1200g (26–42 oz)
20 kg (44 lb)	1000–1600g (35–56 oz)

How to use this guide

- Use the higher end of the range for younger or high-energy pups
- Use the lower end if your dog is nearing adulthood or gains weight easily
- Adjust every 1–2 weeks based on body condition (feel ribs easily = good)

Action Step:

Write down your pup's current weight and how many meals they eat per day. Adjust your meal plan or portions if needed, and don't forget to rotate in a new protein every 10–14 days.

Indi and Evie - playful pups, and below, Evie with Pearl. Note fit, not fat.

Chapter 18

Adults

Maintenance meals

B y the time your dog reaches adulthood, feeding shifts from fuelling growth to supporting balance. You're no longer building the body. You're maintaining it. That means stabilising weight, keeping energy steady, and watching for the first signs of change in digestion, joints, or appetite.

This chapter covers everything you need to feed your adult dog with clarity, confidence, and flexibility, whether you're fully homemade, mix-feeding, or adapting as you go.

What changes at adulthood?

Slower growth = fewer calories needed.
Gut and immune system are more resilient.
Meals shift to 1–2 per day.
Weight management becomes more important than volume

Adult dogs still need:

- High-quality protein

- Healthy fats

- Digestible carbs (if using carbs)

- Fibre and hydration

- Variety across the week

But the goal now is maintenance, not maximum nutrition density every day.

Adult Feeding Guide by Weight

Use this table to estimate daily food needs—**2–3% of body weight**, adjusted for activity level.

Dog Weight (kg / lb)	Daily Food Amount (g / oz)	Breed Examples
2–5 kg (4.4–11 lb)	50–150g (1.75–5.3 oz)	Chihuahua, Maltese, Toy Poodle
6–10 kg (13–22 lb)	150–300g (5.3–10.5 oz)	Mini Schnauzer, Cavalier, Fox Terrier
11–20 kg (24–44 lb)	300–600g (10.5–21 oz)	Border Collie, Cocker Spaniel, Kelpie
21–30 kg (46–66 lb)	600–850g (21–30 oz)	Labrador, Staffy, Bulldog
31–40 kg (68–88 lb)	850g–1.2kg (30–42 oz)	Golden Retriever, Husky, German Shepherd
41–50 kg (90–110 lb)	1.2–1.5kg (42–52.5 oz)	Rottweiler, Doberman, Ridgeback
51kg+ (112lb+)	1.5–2kg+ (52.5–70+ oz)	Great Dane, Mastiff, Wolfhound

Adjusting for real life

Signs you may be feeding too much:

- Weight gain
- Lethargy
- Excessively large stools
- Sluggish digestion

Signs you may be feeding too little:

- Rib and spine prominence
- Low energy
- Excessive begging despite clean meals

Adjust in 10% increments every 1–2 weeks until weight stabilises.

What a balanced adult meal looks like

A typical bowl:

- 50–70% meat (chicken, beef, lamb, turkey, fish)

- 10–20% complex carbs (optional: rice, oats, sweet potato)

- 10–20% veg (steamed or blended)

- Oil, broth, and extras as needed

- Organ meats 1–2x per week (not daily)

Keep it varied over time, but simple in any one meal.

Feeding frequency

1–2 meals per day. *Most adult dogs will thrive very well on 1 feed per day at night.* Picky eaters need several small feeds per day. Large dogs usually need 2 feeds per day to maintain weight. If you're worried your dog is not eating enough, it is OK to top up with kibble.

Have set times, not free-feeding. Add enrichment (lick mats, frozen cubes, treat balls) if you want to slow things down or reduce boredom.

When to re-assess

Even healthy dogs need meal plan check-ins:

- Every 3–6 months, re-weigh your dog. Your vet will usually have a set of scales. Always feed amounts according to ideal weight, not current weight.

- Adjust for seasonal changes (cool weather = more calories)

- Watch for shifts in appetite, coat condition, or stool. These are your first clues

You don't need to recalculate every week, but you *do* need to stay tuned in.

Action Step:

Weigh your dog (actual weight, not a guess!). Check it against the chart above. Are you feeding at the right percentage? Are you seeing the right energy, weight, and stool consistency? If not, adjust. If yes, carry on.

Working dogs need nutrition in keeping with high level demands on their energy.

Chapter 19

Seniors

Joint support, easy digestion and energy

O ld dogs don't need fancy meals. They need comfort, function, and consistency. As your dog moves into his senior years, his nutritional needs begin to shift. Not dramatically, but meaningfully.

This chapter is about feeding older dogs with care, supporting their joints, easing digestion, keeping energy steady, and giving them the nourishment to enjoy their golden years with as much comfort as possible. Because they slow down, they often become overweight. This puts more pressure on their joints.

When is a dog "senior"?

It depends on breed and size.

Dog Size	Senior Age Starts
Small (under 10kg)	10+ years
Medium (10–25kg)	8+ years
Large (25–40kg)	7+ years
Giant (40kg+)	6+ years

But age isn't the only indicator. Look for signs:

- Slowing down or tiring faster

- Stiffness in the morning

- Difficulty chewing harder foods

- Changes in appetite, weight or stools

If you're noticing these things, it's time to adjust meals, gently.

What older dogs need more of

Joint support: Omega-3s, glucosamine, collagen (from bone broth).
Digestibility: Soft foods, fewer ingredients per meal.
Moisture: Older dogs drink less, but still need hydration.
Appetite encouragement: Warm, smelly meals keep interest up.
Consistency: Daily routine matters more than ever:

What they need less of

Calories: Slower metabolism = risk of weight gain.
Hard-to-digest fats: Switch from heavy to light fats (fish over pork).
Raw bones: Dental strength may decline. They may have lost or cracked teeth.
Excess protein: Still important, but in moderation.
Rich treats: One liver-heavy snack can throw off their gut.

How to feed a senior well

Use this base formula (adjusted for size and condition):

- 50–60% gently cooked protein (chicken, turkey, fish, soft lamb)

- 20% mashed veg (pumpkin, carrot, green beans)

- 10–15% soft grain (oats, pearl barley, rice)

- 1 tbsp bone broth

- 1 tsp flax or sardine oil

- Optional: ½ tsp turmeric golden paste or a sprinkle of kelp

Texture matters. Blend if chewing is difficult. Add broth to soften. Serve warm to enhance scent.

Senior-friendly additions

Bone broth: Supports joints, adds hydration, enhances flavour.
Egg yolk: Brain health and digestible fat.
Sardines or fish oil: Anti-inflammatory, supports joints and cognition.
Plain yoghurt or kefir: Gut health and gentle probiotic support.
Pumpkin or chia: Fibre for regular stools.
Turmeric Golden Paste (anti-inflammatory)

Supplements to consider

Before adding anything, talk to your vet. But here's what many senior dogs benefit
from:

- Glucosamine/chondroitin

- Omega-3 fatty acids (EPA/DHA)

- Probiotics

- Vitamin E and C for immune support

You can often get most of these through food, but supplementation can help
bridge the gap if appetite drops.

Keep meals simple, warm and familiar

Older dogs thrive on routine. Sudden changes in texture, temperature, or content
can upset their digestion, or turn them off their bowl entirely.

Use Pearl Barley. It's a gentle, fibre-rich grain that helps digestion and stabilises
energy. Softer and easier to digest than whole barley.

Stick to known favourites. Rotate slowly and carefully, serve warm and feed in a
quiet space. Elevate bowls if posture or joint pain is an issue.

And don't forget to watch body condition. Weight *loss* is just as much a concern
as gain in older dogs.

Action Step:

Make a note of any changes you've noticed in your older dog's energy, digestion, or mobility. Use this to gently adjust their meals over the next two
weeks, one change at a time.

Chicken hearts, beef mince, chick peas, cauliflower rice and broccoli rice, cooked in a wok. Any juices are strained and saved (frozen) for adding to other dishes.

Cook one big batch; store for many easy meals.

Chapter 20

Weight management

Fit, not fat

A few extra kilos on a dog might not seem like much, until you remember they're carrying it on four joints, every hour of the day. Whether your dog's overweight, underweight, or just trending in the wrong direction, this chapter will help you manage their weight safely and sustainably.

No starvation, no fads, just smart feeding, thoughtful adjustments, and a watchful eye.

Why weight matters

Excess weight stresses joints. It increases the risk of diabetes, arthritis, heart and respiratory issues. It shortens lifespan, and impacts comfort long before that.

And yet, underweight dogs aren't healthier. They may lack nutrients, muscle tone, or immune strength.

Know your dog's condition

Use a Body Condition Score (BCS). Think of it as a visual weight chart:

On a scale of 1–9:

- 1–3 = Underweight: Ribs, spine visible; no fat cover

- 4–5 = Ideal: Ribs can be felt but not seen; clear waist

- 6–7 = Overweight: Ribs hard to feel; no waist; belly rounding

- 8–9 = Obese: Heavy fat deposits; movement affected

Quick check: Stand above your dog. Can you see a waist? Run your hands down his ribs. Can you feel them without digging?

For overweight dogs: what to adjust

- Feed 1.5–2% of body weight per day (down from 2.5–3%)

- Stick to lean proteins: chicken breast, white fish, kangaroo, rabbit.

- Use steamed or mashed veg to bulk out meals (zucchini, pumpkin, carrot)

- Limit or remove carbs (rice, oats) and fatty cuts, until weight stabilises.

Activity:

- Add 10 minutes to walks

- Use food puzzles to slow eating

- Add playtime, even in short bursts

Extras to watch:

- Cut treats in half, or swap for steamed veg or a sardine.

- Watch "stealing" for scraps.

- Use training sessions as mealtime. Not as a reason to "add more."

- Separate feeding from other dogs.

Tip: Track weight weekly. Adjust food in 10% increments only.

For underweight dogs: how to build up slowly

- Feed 3–4% of body weight per day

- Add healthy fats: egg yolks, olive oil, fish oil

- Use calorie-dense ingredients: lamb, sardines, eggs, bone broth

- Include small grains: oats, barley, and carbs, like sweet potato

Meals:

- Split into 3 small feeds per day
- Make food smellier and warmer (enhances appetite)

Caution:

- Rule out underlying issues: parasites, dental pain, digestive disorders
- If weight isn't increasing with more food, consult a vet

Sample Lean-Out Bowl (Overweight Dog)

- 100g cooked chicken breast
- ½ cup steamed green beans + pumpkin
- 1 tsp flaxseed oil or sardine
- Sprinkle of ground eggshell

Bulked with fibre, rich in protein, low in carbs, without feeling like a diet.

Sample Bulk-Up Bowl (Underweight Dog)

- 150 ı g lamb mince, chicken livers/hearts, diced pork
- 1 egg yolk
- 1 tbsp bone broth
- 1 tbsp yoghurt

Warm, dense, and nourishing, ideal for slow, steady weight gain.

Action Step:

Weigh your dog this week. Your vet or pet-store usually has a weigh-scale. Take a side-on photo. Then choose one thing to adjust; portion size, treat type, or bowl ingredients. Repeat weekly until you're back in that 4–5/9 BCS zone.

Help other dog owners like you. Leave a quick review!

A huge THANK YOU for picking up "Healthy Dog Food Recipes." I hope it's helping you gain clarity, confidence, and a game plan for your dog's future!

Now, I'd love to ask a small (but meaningful) favour:

Could you take 2 minutes to leave an honest review?
Your feedback does 3 powerful things:

- Helps other enthusiastic dog owners like you discover if this book is right for them.

- Supports me in creating more resources to help people like you succeed.

- Gives you a chance to reflect. What part of the book inspired or helped you most?

Please could you click the universal link below to leave your review on Amazon now:

https://mybook.to/homemade-dog-food

Every single review makes a difference, even just a sentence or two! I am grateful for your support ~ Jeanette

P.S. Already left a review? You're amazing! Consider sharing the book with a friend who'd benefit from it or posting on your Facebook page.

Chapter 21

Working dogs

Feeding for performance and recovery

N ot all dogs spend their days lounging on couches. Some work. And they work hard.

Whether it's herding sheep, assisting police, competing in agility, or covering kilometres on the farm, working dogs burn more fuel, more consistently than the average pet. Feeding them is about *sustaining performance, protecting joints, and speeding recovery.* Always increase calories gradually and seasonally. Working dogs often need more in winter or during heavy work cycles. Their energy output can be 2-4x higher than a typical house pet.

What counts as a working dog?

Herding and farm dogs. (Kelpies, Border Collies, Heelers)
Police, military, and service dogs. (German Shepherds, Malinois, Doberman)
Racing, sport, or agility dogs. (Greyhounds, Whippets, Retrievers)
Hunting or tracking dogs. (Pointers, Spaniels, Hounds, Pig dogs)
Sled dogs, rescue dogs, or even therapy dogs with long work days.

Nutritional needs of a working dog

Higher calorie demands (often 3–5% of body weight in food per day.)
More fat, the best slow-burning fuel for endurance.
Stable protein intake, for muscle recovery and strength.
Hydration and electrolyte balance, critical in heat and hard work.
Joint support and anti-inflammatory foods, to maintain longevity.

What a working dog's dish should include

A daily working ration might look like this (adjust based on season and workload):

- 50–60% protein: lamb, beef, sardines, fish, kangaroo, chicken

- 20–30% fats: meats, sardine oil, eggs, flax or coconut oil

- 10–20% carbs: oats, barley, sweet potato, brown rice. *Barley and oats shine here. They provide slow-release energy with digestible fibre, perfect for sustained work.*

- 5–10% vegetable: for fibre, micro-nutrients, and gut health

- Bone broth, chia, or kefir for hydration and gut support

- Extra egg or sardine after heavy work days

Feeding schedule tips

- Feed 2x daily, or 3x in hot weather or peak seasons

- Post-work meals should be served slightly warm and moist to encourage hydration

- Always feed at least 1 hour before or after intense activity to reduce bloat risk

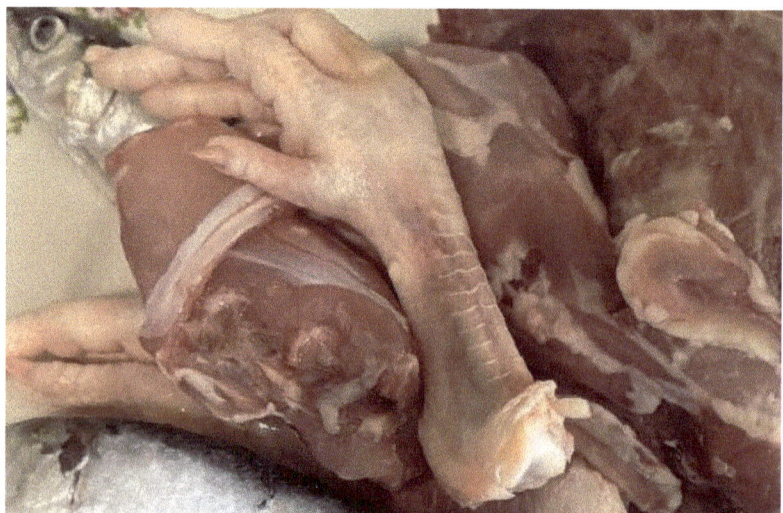

Raw meat, fish and turkey feet for large or working dogs OR cook in a slow cooker.

- Freeze meals in portable containers for days on the road or out on the paddock

Best ingredients for energy and recovery

For Fuel:

- Lamb, beef fat, chicken skin (cooked), coconut oil

- Barley, sweet potato, oats

For muscle repair:

- Beef, kangaroo, turkey, goat, pork

- Sardines, tinned mackerel, eggs

For cooling and rehydration:

- Bone broth ice cubes, goat's milk or kefir (electrolyte support + probiotics)

For joint support:

- Sardine or fish oil

- Turmeric

- Flaxseed

- Bone broth with collagen

Sample plan (for 25kg working dog, moderate workload)

- Breakfast: 300g cooked lamb, ½ cup barley, 1 tbsp coconut oil, ½ cup veg

- Dinner: 250g chicken, ½ sweet potato, 1 boiled egg, broth drizzle

- Add-ins: Sardine or yoghurt cube midday, frozen treat post-work

Target total: ~1kg food/day, high in fat and energy

Watch for these signs:

Thriving:

- Clear eyes, soft coat, firm stools

- High stamina and fast post-work recovery

- Steady weight and strong appetite

Not enough food or imbalance:

- Sudden weight loss, dry coat

- Poor focus or early fatigue

- Excessive licking, eating grass, or weakness

- Changes in gait or reluctance to move

Action Step:

If you have a working dog, calculate their food based on 3–4% of their body weight this week. Track their energy over three days. Adjust fat and protein if you notice changes in performance or recovery.

Working dogs are supreme athletes with stamina.

Chapter 22

Grain-free: Gut health and sensitive stomachs

How to build a stronger gut without guesswork

G rain free doesn't mean carbohydrate free. And it certainly doesn't mean dogs have to miss out on a balanced diet. In the wild, dogs don't graze paddocks of rice or oats, but they do eat partially digested grains and vegetables from the stomach contents of prey animals. So the debate isn't whether dogs can digest some grains. It's about what suits your dog, what's digestible, and what's reliable as a food source.

White rice, for example, is often used in dog meals because it's soft and easy to digest. But it offers very little nutritional value, especially when compared with whole ingredients like quinoa or sweet potato. And some rice, particularly from regions with heavy pesticide use, has been shown to contain small amounts of arsenic or cadmium. Australian-grown rice is cleaner and safer.

Quinoa, on the other hand, is packed with benefits. It has half the carbs of rice, twice the protein, and includes all nine essential amino acids. It's more expensive, and it can cause mild tummy upset in sensitive dogs, especially if not rinsed well or introduced slowly. But it's a strong addition to the rotation if tolerated.

There has been concern around grain-free diets that rely heavily on legumes (like lentils, peas, chickpeas) possibly contributing to heart issues in dogs, specifically dilated cardiomyopathy (DCM). This is still being researched, and it may have more to do with dietary balance than legumes themselves.

Used in moderation, legumes can be a useful source of protein and fibre. They should never be the main protein source, and should be cooked thoroughly and rotated with other ingredients. If you're unsure, speak with your vet, especially if your dog is a breed known to be at risk for heart conditions.

Some dogs seem to digest rocks. Others sniff a new food and end up with three days of gas, mushy stools, or itchy skin. If your dog falls in the second camp, you're not alone, and you're not stuck. This chapter covers what causes sensitive stomachs, how to ease symptoms with real food, and how to slowly build a stronger gut without guesswork.

Signs your dog has gut sensitivities

- Intermittent vomiting (especially yellow bile)

- Diarrhoea or loose stools

- Excess gas or bloating

- Stool inconsistency

- Paw licking or rear-end scooting (There are also other causes for this. Discuss with your vet)

- Poor appetite followed by ravenous eating

- Ongoing itchiness or ear issues without obvious allergy

Common triggers

Too much fat (especially rich cuts or oil overload)
Too much variety, too fast
Overuse of organ meats
Sudden changes in feeding routine
Low-quality treats
Food sensitivities (often chicken, beef, grains particularly wheat, or dairy)

Remember, if you want to be completely grain-free, you can always choose the recipes in this book and leave out the grain in your cooking. Just increase the volume of your meat or veggies.

For grain-free recipes, see Chapter 35.

Gut-supporting ingredients

These foods help settle the digestive tract and support healthy bacteria:

Base ingredients:

- Boiled chicken or turkey
- White rice
- Steamed pumpkin
- Mashed sweet potato
- Bone broth (small amounts)

Soothing additions:

- Slippery elm powder (small doses)
- Chia or flaxseed soaked in water
- Plain, unsweetened yoghurt or kefir
- Tinned pumpkin (not pie filling!)

Fermented options (once stable):

- Sauerkraut (unsalted, raw)
- Fermented veggies
- Goat's milk or kefir ice cubes

The 3-day reset

When symptoms flare up, give the gut a break. Over 3 days, feed small portions 3–4 times/day:

- Boiled white rice
- Boiled chicken or white fish
- Steamed pumpkin
- Optional: bone broth cube, plain yoghurt

Once stools stabilise, reintroduce other foods one at a time, every 2–3 days. Note any reaction.

Longer-term strategy

- Keep meals bland but varied: alternate between 2–3 proteins

- Add fibre slowly: pumpkin, carrot, pearl barley

- Limit fats at first: reintroduce oils and sardines in tiny amounts

- Use probiotics consistently, either through yoghurt/kefir or supplements

- Avoid commercial treats unless they're single-ingredient

- Feed at regular times: gut rhythms respond to routine

A note on food intolerances vs. allergies

- Intolerances = Digestive symptoms: gas, diarrhoea, bloating

- Allergies = Immune symptoms: itchiness, red ears, hives, swelling

Both can be food-related. But true food allergies are rare. Usually it's about quality, quantity, and how food is introduced.

Best foods for sensitive dogs

These ingredients soothe, stabilise, and nourish, perfect for dogs with delicate digestion or recent tummy upsets.

Proteins (low-fat, easily digestible):

Boiled chicken or turkey mince
Tinned fish (sardines, mackerel in water)
White fish or lean lamb
Scrambled or boiled egg

Carbohydrates:

White rice
Sweet potato (cooked, mashed)
Pumpkin (cooked, plain)

Vegetables (blended or mashed):

Carrot
Zucchini
Green beans
Spinach (lightly cooked)

Additions and Soothing Boosters:

Bone broth (gut healing and hydrating)
Yoghurt or kefir (natural probiotics)
Flaxseed or chia (gentle fibre, pre-soaked)
Ginger (natural anti-nausea support)
Turmeric Golden Paste (anti-inflammatory)

Foods to avoid (at least short-term)

Especially during a flare-up or reset period, steer clear of the following:

- Rich meats (liver, pork, fatty beef)

- Dairy, especially milk and cheese

- Gravy, processed toppings, or table scraps

- High-fat treats or "meaty" chews

- Raw bones or unbalanced raw meals (until gut is stable)

- Grains if suspected issues

- Sudden food changes or over-supplementing

Note: Once your dog is stable, some of these can return in moderation. But reintroduce *one at a time* over 2–3 days, always watching stool, energy, and appetite.

Vet check if you notice:

Blood in stool or vomit, weight loss despite eating, ongoing vomiting, pale gums, weakness or sudden severe symptoms.

Homemade food can support recovery, but never replaces urgent care!

Sniper, (Aust Champ Amstafomine Lock N Load) American Staffordshire Terrier, weighing 34 kgs. As an adult he is on a raw food diet. He has raw chicken, including bones, human grade beef mince, fresh lamb and raw beef bones, raw egg and tinned sardines in oil.

Chapter 23

Dental health

Chew-friendly recipes

L et's face it. Dog breath isn't always charming. But beyond the pong, dental health plays a serious role in overall well-being. Plaque, tartar, and gum disease can affect the heart, liver, and kidneys over time.

This chapter shares practical, food-based strategies to keep those teeth clean, without relying solely on vet cleanings or dental chews full of filler.

Why teeth matter

80% of dogs over age 3 show signs of dental disease.
Plaque turns to tartar in 24–48 hours if not removed.
Inflammation in the mouth = inflammation in the body.
Poor dental health can impact appetite, mood, and immunity.

And here's the kicker: most commercial foods *don't* clean teeth. That crunch? It's not enough.

How food supports dental health

- Chewing = cleaning: Bones, firm veg such as raw carrot, and natural chews help scrub plaque.

- Natural enzymes: Found in raw meats and probiotic foods.

- Anti-inflammatory foods: Reduce gum swelling.

- Avoiding sugar and fillers: Cuts down bacterial overgrowth and dental decay.

Feeding real food, cooked or raw, lays the foundation. But a few strategic additions can go further.

Avoid essential oils, which are too concentrated and potentially toxic. Always avoid *wild mints* like pennyroyal. They're toxic to dogs.

Food-based dental boosters

Crunchy veggies:

- Carrot sticks, cucumber, celery

- Freeze for extra firmness

Raw meaty bones: *(Only if appropriate for your dog)*

- Chicken necks, wings, feet (small breeds)

- Lamb ribs, lamb necks or turkey necks, feet (medium/large breeds)

Always supervise. Never feed cooked bones.

Dental-Friendly Treats *(see Part VI):*

- Dehydrated sweet potato slices

- Frozen yoghurt + banana cubes

- Homemade oat + parsley biscuits

Natural Enzymes:

- Raw meat (when feeding raw)

- Yoghurt or kefir

- Coconut oil (antimicrobial properties)

Herbs and Additions:

- Fresh parsley (helps with breath)

- Turmeric (anti-inflammatory)

- Apple cider vinegar (very small amounts in water or broth)

Herbal helpers for oral health

Certain herbs and natural ingredients can support your dog's dental health gently, from the inside out:

Peppermint (fresh leaves only): A small sprinkle of chopped fresh peppermint leaves in food, treats, or frozen cubes can help, being mildly antibacterial and breath-freshening.

Use finely chopped and sparingly in food or treats. It can provide mild nausea relief and be gut soothing (similar to how it works in humans). Not for dogs with liver issues, very small breeds, or sensitive systems.

Parsley: Helps neutralise bad breath and contains chlorophyll, which may help slow bacterial growth in the mouth. Great chopped into meals or baked into treats.

Turmeric: Anti-inflammatory and antioxidant. Supports gum health and may reduce plaque. Pair with coconut oil and a pinch of black pepper for absorption.

Apple cider vinegar:
May help reduce bacteria and tartar buildup. Use just a few drops in broth or water. Not daily, and only if your dog tolerates it well.

These additions won't replace brushing or chewing, but they can support a cleaner, fresher mouth as part of your dog's everyday routine.

When to use caution

Avoid hard, weight-bearing bones (like cow femurs) that can fracture teeth, especially in older or small-breed dogs.

Avoid:

- Synthetic rawhides

- Cooked bones

- Sticky treats or biscuits that coat the teeth

- "Dental chews" with long ingredient lists and sugars

DIY dental routine (no toothbrush needed)

- Include chew-friendly veg several times a week

- Offer a safe raw bone 1–2 times/week if tolerated

- Add a spoon of yoghurt or parsley to meals

- Wipe the gums after meals if dental issues are present

- Get vet checks every 6–12 months

If your dog allows brushing, fantastic. If not, this food-first method still makes a big difference.

Don't forget the teething phase

Between 3 weeks and 6 months, your puppy will go through a full dental change, from 28 baby teeth to 42 adult ones. During this time, chewing becomes essential, not optional.

If puppies don't have appropriate things to chew on, they'll turn to what they can find: shoes, cords, furniture, you, the cat...

Support healthy teething by offering:

- Soft, raw bones (chicken necks or wings) under supervision

- Frozen carrot sticks

- Cold banana slices

- Natural, single-ingredient chews (like dehydrated tendon or fish skins)

This chewing not only soothes their gums and helps loosen baby teeth, but also supports behavioural development and builds lifelong chewing habits that benefit their teeth and jaw. Set them up well now, and you'll likely have fewer dental dramas later.

Action Step:

Pick one dental-friendly habit this week: a carrot stick after dinner, a raw bone trial, or adding parsley to meals. Small changes now mean fewer dental bills later.

Chapter 24

Diet tweaks for anxious dogs

S ome dogs are born with go buttons and no brakes. Others carry tension like a taut leash, even in calm homes. If your dog is overly anxious, excitable, reactive, or just plain *wired*, food might not be the whole solution... but it can help.

This chapter is about supporting your dog's nervous system, gut health, and emotional regulation through what goes in the bowl. Think of it as nutrition with a calming influence.

How food affects behaviour

You've seen it in kids after sugar. Dogs aren't so different.

- Blood sugar spikes can trigger bursts of hyperactivity or restlessness.

- Gut inflammation can influence mood through the gut-brain axis.

- Nutrient deficiencies can reduce serotonin and other calming hormones.

- Overfeeding or over-supplementing can make excitable dogs harder to settle.

That's why behavioural feeding isn't about "sedating" your dog, It's about steadying the system.

Signs your dog may benefit from dietary tweaks

- Excessive licking, chewing paws, or panting

- Inability to relax or lie still for long

- Overreaction to sounds, sights, or touch

- Restlessness after eating

- Difficulty settling at night

- Sudden surges of energy ("zoomies") with no outlet

Behaviour is layered, but if your dog is constantly on edge, their nervous system may be inflamed, overstimulated, or underfed in key areas.

Foods that help calm and stabilise

Calming proteins:

- Turkey (contains tryptophan, helps serotonin production)

- White fish (easy to digest, low in allergens)

- Eggs (rich in calming amino acids)

Complex carbs:

Slow-digesting carbs can help stabilise blood sugar and support steady energy.

- Rolled oats

- Barley

- Sweet potato

- Cooked brown rice (in moderation)

Gut-supportive additions:

The gut and brain are linked, so a calm gut helps a calm mind.

- Bone broth

- Yoghurt or kefir (for probiotics)

- Chia (soothing fibre)

- Pumpkin (easy on the gut, helps regulate digestion)

Natural nervous system helpers:

- Chamomile tea (cooled and added to food in small amounts)
- CBD oil (vet-approved only, not included in this book)

Foods to use cautiously

- High-fat meats (can spike energy, upset digestion)
- Highly processed treats
- Rawhide or synthetic chews
- Overuse of liver or organ meats (can affect mood and metabolism)
- Excess grain-free food with high pea/lentil content (can unbalance nutrients)

Feeding routine matters too

- Stick to structured meal times: predictability = safety for anxious dogs
- Freeze meals or use a lick mat: slows eating, encourages focus
- Warm food slightly: improves smell and interest, encourages calm eating
- Feed early evening, not too close to bed. Avoid post-meal restlessness

Sample calming bowl

- 100g cooked turkey mince
- ½ cup cooked oats
- ¼ cup mashed pumpkin
- 1 tsp yoghurt
- ½ tsp flaxseed
- Splash of cooled chamomile tea

Simple, soft, soothing, and ideal for evenings.

Note on supplements

Some dogs with chronic anxiety benefit from professional support and targeted supplements (like magnesium, L-theanine, or calming herbs). Always consult a vet before introducing anything new, especially if your dog is on medication.

Action Step:

If your dog is anxious or high-energy, replace one meal this week with a calming bowl: oats, turkey, and pumpkin. Add a spoon of yoghurt. Track energy levels, stools, and sleep, for 48 hours. Small shifts can bring big relief.

Sample calming bowl - turkey mince, cooked oats, mashed pumpkin, yoghurt, grated flaxseed.

Part IV

Practical Feeding and Storage

Holly after a big run

Chapter 25

Weekly meal plans for different needs

Y ou've got the ingredients, you understand your dog's needs. Now it's time to pull it all together. Weekly meal plans give you structure without rigidity, variety without overwhelm, and a clear way to stay consistent with feeding.

This chapter includes simple, repeatable weekly plans tailored to different dog types: puppies, adults, seniors, sensitive guts, working dogs, and busy-owner households. All are based on real-world ingredients and realistic prep time.

No perfection, no fancy food charts, just plans that work.

How to use these plans

- Rotate proteins weekly or fortnightly.

- Keep prep days consistent (e.g. Sunday batch cook.)

- Freeze extras in muffin trays or portioned bags.

- Adjust portion size based on weight and condition.

- Introduce new items slowly if your dog is still adapting.

Each plan below is a template, not a rulebook.

Weekly Meal Plan – Puppies

Day	Protein	Carbs	Veg	Extras
Mon	Chicken	Rice	Pumpkin	Yoghurt
Tue	Turkey	Sweet potato	Zucchini	Crushed eggshell
Wed	Sardines	Oats	Spinach	Bone broth
Thu	Beef mince	Pasta	Carrot	Olive oil
Fri	Lamb	Barley	Green beans	Egg yolk
Sat	Chicken + liver	Rice	Broccoli	Parsley
Sun	Restock day	Repeats or soft meals	Soft mash	Kefir

Portion guide: 5–8% body weight/day (divided into 3–4 meals)

Weekly Meal Plan – Adults

Day	Protein	Carbs	Veg	Extras
Mon	Chicken	Brown rice	Zucchini	Flaxseed oil
Tue	Lamb	Barley	Pumpkin	Bone broth
Wed	White fish	Sweet potato	Green beans	Parsley
Thu	Kangaroo	Rice	Spinach	Yoghurt
Fri	Turkey	Oats	Carrot	Olive oil
Sat	Beef	Pasta	Broccoli	Crushed eggshell
Sun	Tinned mackerel	Quinoa	Steamed veg mix	Kefir

Portion guide: 2–3% body weight/day

Weekly Meal Plan – Seniors

Day	Protein	Carbs	Veg	Extras
Mon	Chicken (shredded)	Pumpkin	Carrot mash	Bone broth
Tue	Lamb	Pearl barley (soaked)	Zucchini	Flaxseed
Wed	Sardines	Rice	Spinach (cooked)	Kefir
Thu	White fish	Oats	Green beans	Parsley
Fri	Turkey	Sweet potato	Broccoli (softened)	Olive oil
Sat	Chicken + liver (small)	Pasta	Carrot	Turmeric
Sun	Rest day or blend	Soft mix	Warmed mash	Yoghurt

Portion guide: 1.5–2.5% body weight/day
Tip: Always warm slightly. Serve soft or blended if needed.

Weekly Meal Plan – Working Dogs

Day	Protein	Carbs	Veg	Extras
Mon	Beef	Barley	Zucchini	Egg yolk
Tue	Kangaroo	Sweet potato	Broccoli	Coconut oil
Wed	Chicken + skin	Oats	Carrot	Bone broth
Thu	Tinned mackerel	Rice	Green beans	Flaxseed
Fri	Lamb	Pasta	Spinach	Yoghurt
Sat	Turkey + liver	Rice	Pumpkin	Sardine
Sun	Flexible/prep day	Repeat or rotate	—	Frozen treat

Portion guide: 3–5% body weight/day
Tip: Increase portions on cold or heavy work days.

Weekly Meal Plan – Sensitive Dogs

Day	Protein	Carbs	Veg	Extras
Mon	Boiled chicken	Rice	Pumpkin	Yoghurt
Tue	White fish	Oats	Zucchini	Bone broth
Wed	Turkey	Sweet potato	Carrot	Kefir
Thu	Sardines (in water)	Rice	Green beans	Flaxseed
Fri	Rabbit or lean lamb	Barley	Spinach	Slippery elm
Sat	Chicken (blended)	Soft veg	Blended mash	Probiotic powder
Sun	Simple reset	Rice + pumpkin	None	Chamomile (cooled)

Portion guide: 2–2.5% body weight/day
Tip: No new foods or treats until stable.

Weekly Meal Plan for Busy Households

Cook once, portion twice, top up with store-bought

Day	Morning (kibble)	Evening (homemade)	Topper
Mon	High-protein kibble	Chicken + rice + pumpkin	Kefir
Tue	—	Beef + barley + carrot	Bone broth
Wed	—	Sardines + oats + spinach	Parsley
Thu	—	Turkey + pasta + zucchini	Olive oil
Fri	—	Lamb + sweet potato	Egg yolk
Sat	Treat day	Mix bowl with leftovers	Yoghurt cube
Sun	Kibble	Reset day or cook ahead	Broth + frozen veg

Puppy Feeding Guide by Weight

Puppy Weight (kg / lb)	Daily Food Amount (g / oz)
2 kg (4.4 lb)	100–160g (3.5–5.6 oz)
5 kg (11 lb)	250–400g (8.8–14 oz)
10 kg (22 lb)	500–800g (17.6–28 oz)
15 kg (33 lb)	750–1200g (26–42 oz)
20 kg (44 lb)	1000–1600g (35–56 oz)

Adjust meals weekly as puppies grow quickly. Watch body condition, not just appetite!

Adult Feeding Guide (by Weight)

Use this table to estimate daily food needs—**2–3% of body weight**, adjusted for activity level.

Dog Weight (kg / lb)	Daily Food Amount (g / oz)	Breed Examples
2–5 kg (4.4–11 lb)	50–150g (1.75–5.3 oz)	Chihuahua, Maltese, Toy Poodle
6–10 kg (13–22 lb)	150–300g (5.3–10.5 oz)	Mini Schnauzer, Cavalier, Fox Terrier
11–20 kg (24–44 lb)	300–600g (10.5–21 oz)	Border Collie, Cocker Spaniel, Kelpie
21–30 kg (46–66 lb)	600–850g (21–30 oz)	Labrador, Staffy, Bulldog
31–40 kg (68–88 lb)	850g–1.2kg (30–42 oz)	Golden Retriever, Husky, German Shepherd
41–50 kg (90–110 lb)	1.2–1.5kg (42–52.5 oz)	Rottweiler, Doberman, Ridgeback
51kg+ (112lb+)	1.5–2kg+ (52.5–70+ oz)	Great Dane, Mastiff, Wolfhound

Working dogs, may need 3–4%, while senior or lower-energy dogs may need closer to 1.5–2%.

General notes:

- Puppies (under 6 months): 5–8% of body weight/day

- Adult dogs: 2–3% of body weight/day

- Seniors (7+ years): 1.5–2.5% of body weight/day

- Working dogs: 3–5% of body weight/day

- Weight loss programs: 1.5–2% of body weight/day

Example calculations:

- A 10kg (22lb) adult dog would typically need about 200–300g/ day (7–10.5oz) divided into 1–2 meals.

- A 25kg (55lb) working dog might need 750g/day (1.65lbs/day), possibly more in cold weather.

Action Step:

Pick one template above and customise it for your dog's needs this week. Print it, post it, stick it on the fridge. Whatever suits. You don't need 30 recipes. You need 7 good meals, rotated well.

Lamb mince and pearl barley dish

Chapter 26

Cooking in bulk

Larger meals for multi-dog homes

Feeding in volume: bulk feeding for kennels and multiple dogs

I f you've got five dogs, ten bowls, and one kitchen, you're not cooking for a companion anymore. You're feeding a *pack*. Whether you're running a working kennel, rescue shelter, or simply live on a farm with a chorus of tails at the back door, this chapter is for volume feeders who need efficiency *and* nutrition.

Let's talk about making meals at scale without sacrificing quality or your sanity.

Why bulk feeding?

Saves time.
Reduces cost per meal.
Keeps food consistent across the pack.
Helps monitor weight, condition, and routine.
Encourages a calm, predictable feeding rhythm for your dogs.

Step one: Know your total daily quantity

Use this simple formula:

Total daily feed = 2.5% of each dog's body weight in food

Example

- 5 dogs × avg 20kg × 2.5% = 2.5kg of food/day

- Multiply by 7 days = 17.5kg/week

Factor in working dogs or seniors who may need more or less. Add a buffer for training treats, picky days, or rotating extras.

Step two: Your core recipe for bulk cooking

Ingredient	Metric	Imperial Equivalent
Chicken mince	5 kg	11 lbs
Cooked oats or barley	2 kg	4.4 lbs (approx. 10 cups cooked)
Mixed vegetables *(carrot, zucchini, pumpkin)*	2 kg	4.4 lbs (approx. 9–10 cups chopped/cooked)
Bone broth	1 litre	4¼ cups
Olive oil or flaxseed oil	½ cup	½ cup (120 mL)
Eggs	2 dozen	24 eggs

Note: Supplements (like kelp, turmeric, probiotics, vitamin E, calcium, etc.) should be added at serving time, not stirred through the entire batch, to prevent spoilage and ensure correct dosing per dog. This yields roughly 10–12 kg (22–26 lbs) of finished food. Scale up or down depending on freezer/storage capacity.

Step three: Portion like a pro

Batch cook once a week:

- Use a large stockpot, slow-cooker, or catering pan

- Mix thoroughly for even nutrient distribution

- Cool completely before portioning.

- Portion into total daily requirements: in this example, that would be 2.5kgs/day or 5.1/2 pounds and you would have 7 packs.

Store in:

- Recycled yoghurt tubs or 1L freezer containers.

- Large ziplock bags laid flat (stack like books in your freezer)

Label by date, type, and contents. Store up to 3 days fresh in fridge, 3-4 weeks in freezer

Feeding multiple dogs at once

Use *individual bowls* to monitor intake
Feed calm dogs first, high-anxiety dogs last
If feeding in kennels or crates, pre-portion in labelled tubs
Avoid group feeding unless well-supervised (prevents food guarding and aggression)

Weekly planning

Plan three base batches, each rotated weekly:

Bulk or volume feeds

Plan **three base batches**, each rotated weekly:

Week	Protein	Carb	Veg	Extras
1	Chicken	Oats	Zucchini + pumpkin	Olive oil, sardines
2	Turkey	Rice	Carrot + spinach	Bone broth, eggs
3	Beef	Barley	Green beans + peas	Yoghurt, flaxseed

Why feed calm dogs first?

Feeding calm dogs before high-anxiety or reactive dogs creates a stable, predictable energy in the feeding environment. Feeding anxious or excitable dogs last helps with:

Behaviour regulation

High-anxiety dogs often exhibit:

- Barking

- Pacing

- Guarding or resource defence

- Attempting to steal others' food

By feeding them after the calm dogs are settled, you're:

- Giving them a chance to watch and copy calmer behaviour

- Preventing escalation of excitement or chaos

- Reinforcing calmness = reward (food comes *after* calm)

Pack order reinforcement (for multi-dog homes)

While you don't need to run your home like a wolf den, dogs *do* feel more secure when routine and order are consistent. Feeding the calm dogs first:

- Lowers overall energy

- Shows the anxious dog that they don't need to push or panic to get food

- Helps them build confidence through predictability

Over time, this actually helps reduce *pre-meal anxiety*

Safety

If you have dogs with food-guarding tendencies or competition issues, feeding high-energy or reactive dogs last and separately prevents:

- Bowl snatching

- Fights or tension

- Fast gulping that can lead to bloat or vomiting

Exceptions?

Yes. If an anxious dog calms more quickly with structure, or shows worsening distress when made to wait, you can modify this rule. Some dogs benefit from:

- A separate feeding space

- Being fed *first but alone*, then rejoining the group

As always: follow the dog, not the rule.

Action Step:

If you've got more than 3 dogs, sketch out your weekly batch plan. Choose a base recipe, scale it, and portion it into 3 days' worth of meals. Your dogs will thank you, and your fridge won't ambush you every morning.

Chapter 27

Travel and emergency feeding

What to make in a pinch

T ravel can disrupt everything, including your dog's food routine. Often the dog will reject his favourite food for something more bland or vice versa. But whether you're off for a weekend hike, a holiday road trip, or just visiting family, you don't have to abandon healthy feeding just because you're on the move. This chapter covers how to pack, plan, and portion travel-friendly meals that are simple, safe, and stress-free, for both of you.

Why travel food matters

Keeps digestion consistent.
Prevents upset stomachs from sudden diet changes.
Saves money and stress when options are limited.
Keeps you in control of ingredients.
Helps maintain your dog's training, energy, and comfort.

Before you go: The travel prep checklist

Count how many meals you need (based on portion size × days × dogs)
Choose meals that can be:

- Frozen and thawed

- Served cold or room temp

- Stored in small portions

Prep one or two "emergency meals" with long shelf-life in case of delays.

Best travel-friendly ingredients

Choose meals that:

- Freeze well

- Don't leak or smell too strongly

- Can be mixed and matched

Great proteins:

- Cooked chicken or turkey mince

- Tinned sardines or mackerel (in water)

- Boiled eggs (peeled)

- Dehydrated meats

Great carbs and bulkers:

- Rolled oats

- Mashed sweet potato

- Cooked white rice or barley

- Pre-cooked pumpkin

Great extras:

- Yoghurt pouches

- Broth cubes

- Chia or flaxseed in small jars

- Frozen cubes of blended veg

Storage tips

- Freeze in muffin trays, portable containers: pop out and pack individual serves before leaving

- Use silicone bags or BPA-free pouches: save space and reduce waste

- Label each portion with date and type

- Freeze meals in containers before trips

- Pack a spoon or scoop (you *will* forget otherwise)

Travel coolers or thermal bags work well for day trips. Vacuum flasks keep food cool for several hours. Use frozen meals as "ice bricks" for short trips. They'll defrost gradually and stay cold.

Feeding on the road

- Let frozen meals thaw naturally in a sealed container

- If camping or away from a fridge, serve tinned food + dry cookied carbs (e.g., oats or rice)

- Always pack water + bowl. Hydration matters more than usual during travel

Emergency meal kit (3-day backup)

Keep this in your car or pack:

- 2 tins sardines (in water)

- 1 small jar oats or barley flakes

- 2 eggs (hard-boiled or fresh)

- 1 banana or pouch pumpkin purée

- 1 broth cube or powder sachet

- Ziplock or silicone bowl

- Spoon

In a pinch, that's hydration + protein + carbs + gut support, a solid safety net.

Action Step:

Create your own "Dog Travel Grab Bag" this week. Freeze two muffin trays of food, label a container, and make a checklist. It'll be there next time you pack, and one less thing to think about.

Emergency meals

No food in the fridge? No kibble in the cupboard? The butcher's closed, and the dog's staring at you like, *"This is the worst betrayal I've ever known."* Emergency feeding happens. But that doesn't mean you need to panic, or resort to takeaway sausage rolls.

When You Need This

You ran out of prepped meals.
Your delivery didn't arrive.
You're travelling and forgot food.
There's been a power cut, flood, illness, or life just got in the way.

Pantry staples that can save the day

Safe to feed (plain, cooked or rinsed if tinned):

Proteins:

- Tinned sardines or mackerel (in spring water)

- Eggs (boiled or scrambled)

- Plain tinned chicken (low sodium)

- Leftover roast meat (unseasoned, no gravy)

- Plain cooked lentils (in small amounts)

Carbs and Fillers:

- Rolled oats (soak in hot water for 10 mins)

- White rice or brown rice

- Mashed pumpkin or sweet potato

- Plain cooked pasta

- Barley or couscous

Veggies:

- Frozen carrots, peas, green beans (rinsed and steamed)

- Tinned pumpkin (no pie spice!)

- Fresh zucchini, spinach, or broccoli (lightly steamed)

Toppers (if available):

- Bone broth cubes

- Yoghurt or kefir

- Chia or flaxseed (soaked)

- Olive oil or flaxseed oil

- Parsley or turmeric

3-Minute emergency meal ideas

The One-Pan Scramble

- 1 egg

- ½ cup oats

- ½ cup frozen peas or pumpkin
  Cook gently until soft and serve warm.

The "Leftover Bowl"

- ½ cup leftover roast chicken or beef

- ½ cup rice or pasta

- Small scoop of yoghurt

- Sprinkle of parsley

The Pantry Mix

- 1 tin sardines (rinsed)

- 1 cup oats soaked in warm water

- ¼ cup mashed veg

- 1 tsp ground flaxseed

The Bare Minimum (Still Better Than Kibble)

- 1 boiled egg

- 1 tbsp cooked rice or oats

- 1 tsp oil
  Mix and serve with water.

All of these are:

- Suitable for most dogs

- Easily digestible

- Customisable with herbs, veggies, or broth

Note:

- If feeding as a treat, topper, or light meal, reduce their regular portion that day to avoid overfeeding.

- You can always bulk up with extra veggies or oats for dogs with big appetites but lower activity.

- These recipes are not intended to be full-time meals for every dog. They work well in rotation or as flexible options when you're short on time or groceries.

Quick freeze tip

Freeze 2–3 portions of an "emergency blend" next time you cook. Use:

- Chicken or sardines

- Rice or oats

- Veg mash

- Bone broth cubes

Store flat in labelled freezer bags = peace of mind later.

Action Step:

Make one emergency portion this week. Label it "EMERGENCY" and freeze it. Add one tin of sardines and a small bag of oats to your pantry. You're now officially prepared.

Part V

Natural Health Boosts and Remedies

Evie imitating a kangaroo

Chapter 28

Everyday health boosts

Herbs, oils and bone broth

S ome of the most powerful health tools don't come in tablets or vet-prescribed powders. They're right in your kitchen; fresh, everyday ingredients that gently boost immunity, reduce inflammation, aid digestion, and add depth to your dog's diet. This chapter is a calm, confident guide to natural "boosters" you can stir, spoon, or blend into meals with ease. And best of all, they're usually already in your pantry or fridge.

Why use boosters?

Fill nutritional gaps
Support gut health and joint function
Reduce inflammation
Freshen breath and coat
Improve appetite and digestion
Rotate for variety without overhauling meals

Bone broth: liquid gold

Benefits:

- Joint support (rich in collagen, glucosamine)

- Gut healing and hydration

- Helps picky eaters or those recovering from illness

How to use:

- Drizzle over meals (1–2 tbsp per 10kg dog)

- Warm gently to enhance appetite

Bone Broth

- 1–1.5 kg (2–3 lbs) of bones (chicken frames, beef marrow bones, turkey necks, etc.)

- 3–4 litres (approx. 12–16 cups) of water

- A splash (1–2 tbsp) of apple cider vinegar

Simmer for 12–24 hours.

You'll typically get: 2.5 to 3 litres of finished broth, (about 10–12 cups) depending on evaporation and fat content.) The bones break down slightly, some liquid evaporates, and the final yield depends on how tightly you cover the pot, the cooking time, and whether you remove any foam/fat during the process.

Freezing tip by volume:

- Ice cube tray: ~1 tbsp (15ml) per cube

- Muffin tray: ~½ cup (120ml) per muffin

- Small glass jars: 1–2 cups (240–480ml) per portion

This makes it super easy to portion out broth by dog size or meal need. Strain and cool. Store 3 days in fridge, 2 weeks in freezer.

Oils: For shine, brain, and balance

Flaxseed Oil: Source of omega-3 (plant-based). Great for dry skin, mild inflammation

Sardine or Fish Oil: Brain, skin, and joint support. Rich in EPA/DHA

Olive Oil: Antioxidant and anti-inflammatory. Helps with coat and digestion.

Coconut oil: also excellent

Use ½–1 tsp per 10kg body weight, 2–3 times a week. Too much can lead to loose stools or weight gain.

Herbs: Gentle, natural support

Parsley:
Freshens breath, rich in vitamin K. Use chopped, fresh, small pinches over meals

Peppermint (fresh leaves):
Mild antimicrobial, aids digestion and breath. Use sparingly. No essential oil!

Turmeric:
Anti-inflammatory and antioxidant. Pair with a drop of oil and a pinch of pepper for absorption

Ginger (fresh or powdered):
Eases nausea, supports digestion. Good for travel days or sensitive tummies

Chamomile (cooled tea):
Soothing and calming. Add a spoon to evening meals

Seeds and supplements

Chia Seeds:
Good fibre and omega-3. Soak before feeding. 1 tsp per 10kg max

Collagen: How do you add collagen? Use chicken feet, fish skin, or powdered collagen supplements. Start with small amounts.

Hemp Seeds (moderate):
Protein, omegas, and anti-inflammatory. Use cautiously, high fat content. (Not covered in this book.)

Pumpkin Seeds: (Pepitas)
Natural de-wormer, rich in zinc and antioxidants. Use ground or finely chopped

---

Action Step:

Rotate one or two boosters per week. Overloading too many at once can confuse your dog's gut, and your feeding routine. Watch for changes in coat, digestion, or energy.

Bonus Chapter – *If you would like a bonus chapter on natural recipes for minor issues, just email me at jeanette.gower@gmail.com with Bonus Chapter in the heading and I can send it to you.*

Zoomies by Holly

Chapter 29

Supplementing the natural way

(when needed)

Y ou don't need a drawer full of powders to feed your dog well. In fact, most healthy dogs on a balanced, homemade diet need very few supplements at all.

But there are times when a thoughtful, natural addition can make all the difference, especially for dogs with specific needs, dietary gaps, or age-related concerns.

When might a dog need a supplement?

Homemade meals aren't yet fully balanced
Specific health condition (joints, anxiety, gut trouble)
Older age = slower absorption
Recovery from illness or surgery
Selective eaters with patchy intake

If your meals are balanced over time, and your dog is thriving, *you may not need any at all.*

Signs you might have a nutrient gap

- Dull coat or skin flaking

- Ongoing loose stools

- Poor appetite or slow recovery

- Joint stiffness or reluctance to move

- Repeated ear infections or itchiness

- Excess shedding or brittle nails

Always rule out bigger health issues with your vet before supplementing on guesswork.

Commonly helpful, naturally sourced supplements

Calcium (if you're not feeding bones)

- Why: Bone growth, muscle contraction, nerve health

- Natural sources: Crushed eggshell (1 tsp = 800–1,000 mg)

- When needed: if feeding boneless cooked or raw meals long-term

Making your own calcium powder from eggshells

- Rinse your eggshells well.

- Then spread them out on a tray and bake in a low oven, around 110°C (225°F), for 20 minutes, to ensure they're completely dry and brittle.

- Once cooled, grind them into a very fine powder. A spice or coffee grinder works best for a smooth, flour-like finish, though a food processor or blender will also do the job if that's what you have.

- Store in a dry jar and use in small, measured amounts.

Omega-3 fatty acids (EPA/DHA)

- Why: Reduces inflammation, supports joints, skin, brain

- Natural sources: Sardines, mackerel, fish oil

- Dose: 100–200 mg EPA/DHA per 5kg body weight daily

- Signs of deficiency: Dull coat, skin flaking, joint stiffness

Glucosamine and Chondroitin

- Why: Joint repair and mobility

- Natural sources: Bone broth, green-lipped mussel powder, chicken feet

- Use for: Older dogs, large breeds, arthritis-prone pups

Probiotics

- Why: Gut balance, immune function, stool consistency
- Natural sources: Plain yoghurt, kefir, fermented veg
- Best for: Dogs recovering from antibiotics, sensitive stomachs, anxiety

Vitamin B Complex

- Why: Energy metabolism, nervous system, stress support
- Natural sources: Liver (in moderation), eggs, green veg
- When to add: Older dogs, anxious dogs, fussy eaters

Turmeric (Curcumin is the active ingredient)

- Why: Anti-inflammatory, antioxidant
- How to use: ¼ tsp turmeric + dash of oil + pinch of black pepper
- Best for: Arthritis support, skin flare-ups, general ageing

Superfoods

You can sprinkle 1/2 teaspoon of spirulina, kelp or powdered green-lipped mussel over meals, but amounts vary according to the weight of the dog. Dosages will be on the bottle. Beware of overdosing. These provide minerals, anti-oxidants and anti-inflammatory support.

Supplements to be careful with

Too much calcium: can interfere with phosphorus and cause joint issues
Excess vitamin A (from too much liver): risk of toxicity
Iron, zinc, and copper: only supplement under veterinary guidance
Multiple "all-in-one" powders: often expensive, redundant, or unbalanced

A food-first mindset

Food is still the foundation. Supplements should fill in, not take over.

Try to meet needs through ingredients first:

- Eggs = B vitamins + choline

- Yoghurt = probiotics + calcium

- Pumpkin seeds (cooked) = zinc + fibre

- Broth = joint support

- Liver = vitamins A and B12 (in *small* amounts)

Other culinary herbs and spices with safe, functional uses for dogs in very small amounts:

- Ginger: Can help soothe nausea and aid digestion. Use a small pinch grated or powdered.

- Black pepper: Only in minuscule amounts and generally not necessary unless using turmeric.

- Rosemary: Contains antioxidants and is sometimes used as a natural preservative. Use fresh leaves or dried, finely crushed. A small pinch only.

- Oregano: Antibacterial and anti-fungal in small doses. Strong in flavour and should be used sparingly.

Never use essential oils or concentrated herbal extracts unless prescribed. When in doubt, stick with fresh or dried kitchen herbs in tiny amounts. Always observe your dog's reaction when introducing something new.

Only supplement after you assess what's already in the bowl.

Action Step:

Review your current meal plan. Are you feeding bones? Is your dog showing signs of gut imbalance or joint issues? Add *one* natural source of support this week, like yoghurt, fish oil, or bone broth, and track any changes.

Bonus Chapter – *If you would like a bonus chapter on natural recipes for minor issues, just email me at jeanette.gower@gmail.com with Bonus Chapter in the heading and I can send it to you.*

Part VI

Recipes

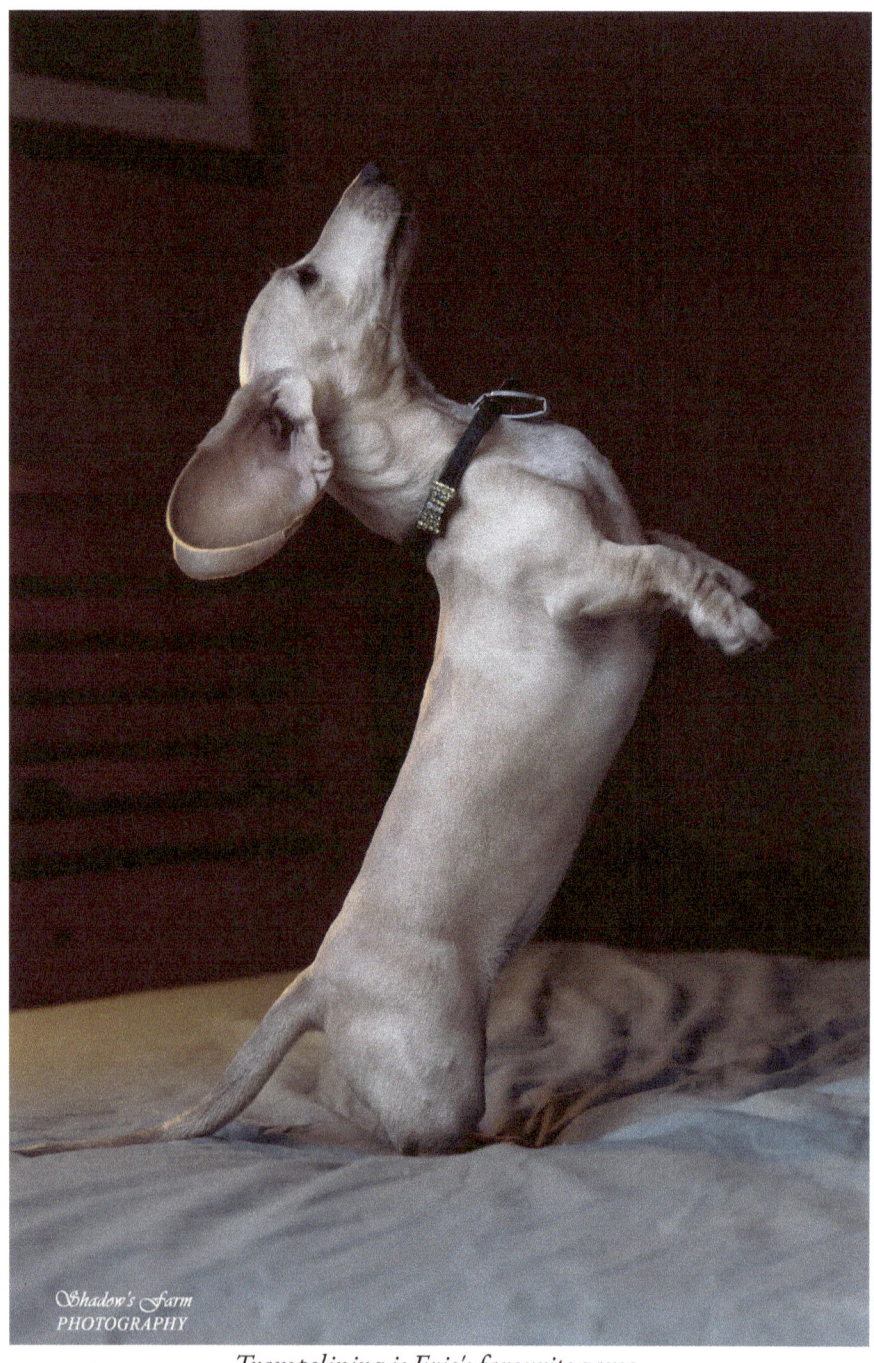

Trampolining is Evie's favourite game.

Chapter 30

Everyday mains

Chicken, beef, lamb, fish, vegetables

W holesome, simple meals for every day. These recipes are designed for real-life feeding: busy mornings, evening routines, or anytime you want to know your dog is getting clean, complete nourishment.

Each meal is simple, adaptable, and budget-friendly, featuring easy-to-find ingredients you can tweak depending on season or what's in your fridge. You can double or even triple the ingredients for larger dogs, or more portions.

Lamb and Mushroom Stew

- 1½ cups diced lamb (shoulder or lean cut)
- ¼ cup cooked button mushrooms, finely chopped
- ½ cup cooked rolled oats
- ¼ cup pumpkin puree
- 1 tsp coconut oil
- 2 tbsp bone broth

Instructions:

- Brown lamb in broth. Add mushrooms and oats. Simmer until soft. Stir in pumpkin and oil. Cool before serving.

Best for: ideal for cool days, hearty and warming

Chicken and Pumpkin Comfort Bowl

- 1 cup cooked chicken breast (shredded or finely diced)

- ½ cup cooked plain pumpkin (mashed)

- ¼ cup cooked white rice

- 1 teaspoon olive oil or flaxseed oil

Instructions:

- Mix all ingredients together until smooth and warm slightly if refrigerated. Serve at room temperature.

Best For: Sensitive tummies, senior dogs, puppies transitioning to solids

Beef and Barley Strength Bowl

- ½ cup lean beef mince (lightly browned, no seasoning)

- ½ cup cooked pearl barley

- ¼ cup diced carrot (cooked)

- ¼ cup chopped green beans (cooked)

Instructions:

- Mix all ingredients well and cool before serving. Optional: Add a dash of bone broth for extra joint support.

Best For: Active dogs needing sustained energy

Sardine and Sweet Potato Power Mix

- 1 tin sardines in water (drained)

- ½ cup cooked mashed sweet potato

- 2 tablespoons rolled oats (cooked soft)

- 1 tablespoon plain yoghurt

Instructions:

- Mash sardines with sweet potato and oats. Stir through the yoghurt before serving.

Best For: Skin and coat health, brain support (DHA!)

Turkey and Spinach Energy Meal

- 1 cup cooked turkey mince

- ½ cup cooked brown rice

- ¼ cup steamed spinach (cooled, finely chopped)

- 1 teaspoon flaxseed oil

Instructions:

- Mix turkey, rice, and spinach. Drizzle oil just before serving.

Best For: Weight management, anxious or high-energy dogs (turkey = calming)

Chicken and Cauliflower Dish

- 1½ cups cooked chicken breast, chopped

- ¼ cup steamed cauliflower, finely chopped

- ½ cup cooked brown rice

- 2 tbsp grated carrot

- 1 tsp olive oil

- Splash of bone broth

Instructions:

- Mix all ingredients gently while warm. Let cool to room temperature. Serve as a full meal or over kibble.

Best for: Great for sensitive stomachs and high-fibre support

Beef and Tomato Grain-free Mix

- 1 cup cooked beef mince
- ¼ cup ripe red tomato (peeled, seeded, diced)
- ½ cup mashed sweet potato
- ¼ cup steamed green beans
- 1 tsp flaxseed oil
- Pinch of chopped parsley

Instructions:

- Cook beef and tomato together lightly. Add sweet potato and green beans. Stir in oil and parsley after cooling.

Best for: dogs avoiding grains or needing high iron and flavour

Tuna and Cucumber Summer Bowl

- 1 tin tuna in spring water, drained
- ¼ cup cucumber, peeled and finely diced
- ½ cup cooked white rice
- ¼ cup zucchini
- 1 tsp olive oil
- 1 tbsp natural yoghurt (optional)

Instructions:

- Mix tuna with rice and vegetables. Add cucumber and yoghurt last. Serve chilled or room temperature.

Best for: Cooling and light, ideal for summer or sensitive tummies

Turkey and Bok Choy Stir-up

- 1 cup cooked turkey mince
- ¼ cup finely chopped bok choy (steamed)
- ½ cup cooked quinoa
- ¼ cup diced carrot
- 1 tsp sesame oil (optional) or flaxseed oil

Instructions:
Stir all ingredients gently. Allow to cool. Add oil last.

Best for: Suitable as a meal or topper. Simple and full of gentle greens.

Rabbit and Rice Allergy-Friendly Bowl

- 1 cup cooked rabbit meat, or substitute (boneless, shredded)
- ½ cup cooked white rice
- ¼ cup blended carrot and zucchini mash
- 1 tablespoon plain kefir

Instructions:

- Mix all ingredients gently. Feed freshly made or portion and freeze.

Best For: Dogs with food sensitivities, elimination diets

Note for all everyday mains:

- Portion sizes depend on your dog's weight. Refer back to your daily feeding guide.
- Store fresh meals for up to 3 days in fridge, or freeze in muffin trays for small-serve portions.

Tuna and cucumber summer bowl.

Chapter 31

Raw food combos

E asy, balanced ideas. These raw meals are gentle, approachable, and a great starting point if you're curious about feeding raw without jumping into complicated formulas.

Turkey Neck and Veggie Mash

- 1 small raw turkey neck (suitable for dog size)
- ½ cup blended carrot and zucchini mash
- 1 teaspoon flaxseed oil

Instructions:

- Serve the turkey neck whole (supervised!) alongside the veggie mash.
- Drizzle a little oil over the veggies.

Best for: Dental health, natural chewing instinct

Lamb Mince Power Bowl

- ½ cup raw lamb mince
- 1 egg (raw, optional)
- ¼ cup steamed spinach (cooled)
- 1 tablespoon pumpkin puree

Instructions:

- Combine lamb, spinach, and pumpkin.
- Crack a raw egg over the top if your dog tolerates it.

Best for: Muscle building, iron boost

Sardine and Green Bean Crunch

- 1–2 raw sardines (fresh or frozen, thawed)
- ½ cup green beans (lightly cooked and cooled)
- 1 teaspoon coconut oil

Instructions:

- Place sardines and green beans together.
- Drizzle with coconut oil just before feeding.

Best for: Omega-3 support, joint health

Goat and Sweet Potato Gentle Start

- ½ cup raw ground goat meat
- ¼ cup mashed cooked sweet potato
- 1 tablespoon kefir or plain yoghurt

Instructions:

- Mix goat meat with sweet potato.
- Stir kefir through at serving time.

Best for: Sensitive stomachs, novel protein introduction

Rabbit and Broccoli Bright Bowl

½ cup raw rabbit meat (boneless)

¼ cup finely chopped steamed broccoli

1 teaspoon fish oil

Instructions:

- Combine meat and broccoli gently.

- Add fish oil just before serving.

Best for: Dogs needing extra selenium and B vitamins

Important raw feeding notes:

- Introduce raw meals gradually over 7–10 days if your dog is switching from kibble.

- Always supervise when feeding bones.

- Source all meats from reputable suppliers. No supermarket clearance trays for raw feeding! (Cook only).

Dehydrated beef strips (see p 197).

Bonus: Build-your-own BARF meal

BARF = "Biologically Appropriate Raw Food," or sometimes "Bones And Raw Food."

Basic BARF Ratio:

Ingredient Group	% of Bowl
Raw meaty bones (edible size)	40–50%
Raw muscle meat	30–40%
Raw organ meat (liver, kidney)	10%
Blended veggies + seeds	10%

How to build it:

- Pick one meaty bone: e.g., chicken wing, turkey neck, lamb riblet

- Add a slab of muscle meat: e.g., beef mince, goat chunks, turkey thigh

- Add a spoon of organ meat: e.g., chopped liver, kidney, spleen

- Add a small veggie blend: e.g., carrot, spinach, green beans, pumpkin (lightly steamed and pureed)

Optional boosters:

- Sardines or mackerel

- Raw egg (yolk preferred)

- Kefir or yoghurt splash

- Chia or flax seeds (soaked)

Golden BARF tips:

- Bones must be raw, not cooked!

- Always match bone size to your dog. Small dogs = small soft bones; big dogs = bigger edible bones.

- Rotate proteins for variety, but introduce slowly.

Chapter 32

Slow-cooker favourites

Set and forget

There's something steadying about a slow-cooked meal. It fills the house with purpose. It tells you you've done enough. That your dogs will be fed for the next few days and you don't need to reinvent anything. For those days when life's a little chaotic (or you just want dinner ready without thinking), slow-cooker meals are a gift. These recipes are nutrient-dense, low fuss, and perfect for batch cooking and freezing.

Slow-cooking for the week ahead

We're using:

- Your slow-cooker or large stock pot

- Common, affordable ingredients

- No-fuss methods that take 15 minutes to prep, not 45

- Yields that freeze well and suit small to giant dogs

Each of the following recipes makes approximately 5 to 6 kilograms (11 to 13 pounds) of finished food. That's enough for one week of main meals for a medium or large dog, or to use as a base meal for multiple dogs.

Slow-cooker basics

How to batch without burnout.

- Cook on low for 6 to 8 hours, or high for 3 to 4 hours

- Chop vegetables large for chunkiness, or small if you plan to mash

- Stir in oils and sensitive ingredients like yoghurt or supplements *after* cooking

- Cool fully before freezing. Portion into containers by day servings, or 3-day thawing in the fridge.

- Always label what's in it and the date

Portion guide (per meal)

Dog Size	Weight Range	Approximate Recipe Portion
Toy/Small Dog	under 5–8 kg / 11–17 lb	½ of any recipe per meal
Medium Dog	9–20 kg / 20–44 lb	1 full recipe (as a light meal)
Large Dog	21–40 kg / 45–88 lb	1½ to 2x recipe (or serve as a topper)
Giant Dog	40+ kg / 88+ lb	2x+ recipe or use as snack/top-up

Weekly ingredient amounts (per dog)

Large dog (30 to 45 kg):

- 2.5 to 3 kg meat (mince, chunks, or bone-in like turkey necks)

- 1.5 kg carbs (rice, oats, barley, sweet potato or lentils)

- 1 to 1.2 kg vegetables (e.g. pumpkin, carrot, zucchini, green beans)

- 500 ml bone broth or water

- ¼ cup oil (olive, flaxseed or coconut)

- Optional: 1 tsp calcium or egg shell powder, and 1 tbsp chopped parsley

Small dog (5 to 10 kg):

- 800 g (28.24 oz) meat
- 500 g (28.24 oz) carbs
- 400 g (14.12 oz) vegetables
- 1 to 2 tbsp oil
- Optional: Small pinch of calcium powder or ½ tsp ground flax

The recipes

These are based on a medium sized dog to last one week.

Lamb and Barley Stew

- 2.5 kg (5.51 lb) lamb (shoulder, neck or mince)
- 1.5 kg (5.51 lb) cooked pearl barley
- 500 g pumpkin (17.65 oz) pumpkin, cubed
- 400 g (14.12 oz) zucchini, diced
- 300 g (10.59 oz) carrot, grated
- 500 ml (16.9 fl oz) bone broth or water
- ¼ cup olive oil

Chicken and Pumpkin Mash

- 2 kg (4.41 lb) chicken thighs or mince
- 1.5 kg (3.31 lb) sweet potato, peeled and chopped
- 500 g (17.65 oz) pumpkin purée
- 400 g (14.12 oz) peas or green beans
- 500 ml (16.9 fl oz) water

- 2 tbsp flaxseed oil

Fish and Root Vegetable Medley

- 1.5 kg (3.31 lb) white fish or tinned salmon (in water)
- 1.5 kg (3.31 lb) cooked rice
- 300 g (10.59 oz) carrots
- 300 g (10.59 oz) parsnip or beetroot, cooked
- 200 g (7.06 oz) spinach, chopped
- 1 tbsp coconut oil

Beef, Oats and Veggie Stew

- 2 kg (4.41 lb) lean beef mince or chunks
- 1.5 kg (3.31 lb) cooked rolled oats
- 400 g (14.12 oz) broccoli, chopped
- 300 g (10.59 oz) green beans
- 300 g (10.59 oz) pumpkin
- 500 ml (16.9 fl oz) bone broth
- 2 tbsp olive oil

Egg and Lentil Budget Base

- 2 dozen eggs, chopped or scrambled
- 1.5 kg (3.31 lb) cooked lentils
- 1 kg (2.2 lb) cooked oats
- 300 g (10.59 oz) peas

- 300 g (10.59 oz) grated carrots
- 1 tbsp apple cider vinegar
- 1 tbsp flaxseed oil

Mixed Meat and Veggie Boost

- 1.5 kg (3.31 lb) mixed meat (e.g. lamb and beef)
- 500 g (17.65 oz) tinned sardines (in water, drained)
- 1.5 kg (3.31 lb) sweet potato
- 400 g (14.12 oz) carrots
- 300 g (10.59 oz) zucchini
- 500 ml (16.9 fl oz) water
- 1 tbsp ground flaxseed
- 1 tbsp coconut oil

Recipes for Smaller Dogs

Beef and Vegetable Slow Stew

- 500g (17.65 oz) lean beef mince or stewing beef, cubed
- 1 cup chopped pumpkin
- 1 cup chopped carrot
- 1 cup chopped zucchini
- ½ cup cooked barley
- 2 cups water or low-sodium bone broth

Instructions:

- Layer beef and vegetables in the slow-cooker.

- Pour water or broth over the top.

- Cook on low for 6–8 hours or high for 3–4 hours, until tender.

- Cool before serving.

Best for: Active dogs, meal prepping for the week

Chicken and Oats Comfort Stew

- 2 skinless chicken thighs (boneless)

- 1 cup rolled oats (added halfway through cooking)

- 1 cup diced sweet potato

- 1 cup green beans

- 2 cups water

Instructions:

- Place chicken and sweet potato in the slow-cooker with water.

- After 2 hours on low, stir in oats and green beans.

- Continue cooking another 2–3 hours.

- Shred chicken before serving.

Best for: Gentle digestion, calming meals for nervous dogs

Fish and Rice Soothing Stew

- 2 white fish fillets (e.g., cod or whiting)
- 1 cup cooked white rice
- 1 cup chopped spinach
- 1 tablespoon flaxseed or fish oil (added after cooking)
- 2 cups water

Instructions:

- Place fish and spinach into slow-cooker with water.
- Cook on low for 2–3 hours.
- Stir in cooked rice at the end.
- Cool slightly and mix in the oil before serving.

Best For:

- Sensitive stomachs, omega-3 boost

Lamb and Barley Strength Casserole

- 500g (17.65 oz) lamb mince or diced lamb shoulder
- 1 cup cooked pearl barley
- 1 cup diced carrot
- ½ cup peas
- 2½ cups water or bone broth

Instructions:

- Brown lamb lightly (optional for better flavour).
- Place lamb, carrots, and peas into the slow-cooker.
- Add water/broth and cook on low for 6–8 hours.

- Stir in cooked barley before serving.

Best for: Dogs needing higher iron and muscle support

Turkey and Pumpkin Recovery Stew

- 500g ground turkey
- 1 cup pureed pumpkin
- 1 cup cooked white rice
- 1 cup chopped zucchini
- 2 cups water or light bone broth

Instructions:

- Combine all ingredients except pumpkin in slow-cooker.
- Cook on low for 5–6 hours.
- Stir in pumpkin puree before cooling and serving.

Best for: Post-illness recovery, gut-soothing meal option

Notes for all slow-cooker meals:

- Portion into 3-day fridge supplies or freeze in silicone trays.
- Always cool food to room temperature before freezing or feeding.
- Adjust water levels depending on stew or thickness preference.

Chapter 33

Roasted favourites

Cook with your own meals if you wish

Here are three dog-friendly roasted recipes that offer flavour, texture, and variety while sticking to safe, balanced ingredients. Each is portioned for a medium dog (15–25 kg) over 2–3 days, and can be scaled up or down as needed.

Roasted Lamb and Pumpkin

- 800 g (1.75 lb) lamb shoulder or leg, diced
- 400 g (14 oz) pumpkin, cubed
- 200 g (7 oz) zucchini, chopped
- 1 tbsp olive oil
- ½ cup cooked rice or oats (optional)
- 1 tsp crushed eggshell powder or calcium supplement

Instructions:

- Preheat oven to 180°C (350°F).
- Place lamb and vegetables in a roasting tray. Toss lightly in olive oil.
- Roast for 35–40 minutes, turning halfway, until meat is cooked and veg are soft.
- Cool slightly, then mix with rice and calcium.

- Store in fridge for up to 3 days or freeze in portions.

Roast Goat and Vegetables

- 800 g (1.75 lb) goat meat (bone-in shoulder or diced)

- 300 g (10.5 oz) sweet potato, peeled and cubed

- 200 g (7 oz) green beans, ends trimmed

- 1 tbsp olive oil

- ½ cup cooked pearl barley or oats

- 1 tsp calcium powder or crushed eggshell (optional)

Instructions:

- Preheat oven to 180°C (350°F).

- Arrange goat meat and vegetables in a roasting tray. Drizzle with olive oil.

- Roast for 45–50 minutes, or until the meat is tender and veg are soft.

- Let cool slightly, de-bone if necessary, and mix with barley or oats and calcium.

- Serve in portions. Refrigerate for up to 3 days or freeze.

Roast Chicken and Mash

- 1 kg (2.2 lb) chicken thighs , boneless and skinless

- 2 carrots, peeled and halved

- 1 small sweet potato, cubed

- 1 tbsp flaxseed oil or olive oil

- ½ cup cooked lentils or barley

- 1 tbsp chopped parsley (optional)

Instructions:

- Roast chicken and root veg at 180°C (350°F) for 30–35 minutes.

- Remove bones and chop or shred chicken.

- Mash carrots and sweet potato together.

- Combine everything with lentils and parsley.

- Serve warm or cool, and refrigerate extras.

Baked Fish and Veggie Mix

- 600 g (1.3 lb) white fish fillets (cod, barramundi, or basa)

- 1 small beetroot, peeled and chopped

- 1 zucchini or half a small broccoli head, chopped

- 1 tbsp coconut oil

- 1 cup cooked quinoa

- 1 tsp ground flaxseed or kelp powder

Instructions:

- Line a baking tray with aluminium foil. Lay out fish and veg, drizzle with coconut oil and wrap in the foil.

- Roast at 180°C (350°F) turning once, for 25 minutes or until fish flakes easily.

- Mix with quinoa and flax or kelp.

- Portion and refrigerate or freeze as needed.

Roasted chicken drumsticks with barley and spinach. Strain and remove bones before feeding out.

Chapter 34

Grain-free options

G rain free doesn't mean nutrient-poor or flavourless. These recipes are built around whole proteins, gentle vegetables, and healthy fats. They are ideal for dogs with grain sensitivities, allergies, or those who simply thrive better on lower-carb meals.

In this chapter, you'll find simple, nutritious grain free meals that rely on root vegetables, meats, seeds, and a little kitchen common sense. Try a few, and trust what works best for your dog.

Instructions: Combine all ingredients, cool before serving. Serve fresh or store in portions.

Pork and Root Vegetable bowl

- 1½ cups cooked pork (boneless, lean cuts)

- ½ cup mashed sweet potato

- ¼ cup chopped carrot (steamed)

- 1 tbsp flaxseed oil

- 1 tbsp bone broth

Lamb and Green Bean Sauté

- 1½ cups cooked lamb mince

- ½ cup diced green beans (lightly steamed)

- ¼ cup pumpkin purée
- 1 tsp olive oil
- Pinch of parsley (optional)

Beef and Cauliflower Mash

- 1½ cups lean ground beef
- ½ cup steamed cauliflower (mashed)
- ¼ cup grated zucchini
- 1 tsp flaxseed oil
- 2 tbsp bone broth

Pepita and Chicken Blend

- 1 cup cooked chicken breast, chopped
- 2 tbsp toasted, ground pepitas
- ½ cup diced carrots
- ¼ cup steamed broccoli
- 1 tsp coconut oil

Lamb Liver and Veggie Boost

- 1 cup lamb liver, chopped and lightly sautéed
- ¼ cup grated carrot
- ½ cup cooked sweet potato
- 1 tsp ground flaxseed
- Splash of water or bone broth for mixing.

Chapter 35

Bulk recipes

E ach makes approximately 5kgs (11 lbs) of finished food. All are balanced, flexible, and freezer-friendly.

Each feeds approximately 10-12 large dog meals, or more if used as a topper.

Chicken and Oat Stew

Yields: ~5 kg / 11 lbs

Ingredient	Metric	Imperial
Chicken mince (or thighs, chopped)	2.5 kg	5.5 lbs
Cooked oats	1.5 kg	3.3 lbs (approx. 7 cups)
Carrots, grated	500 g	1.1 lbs (approx. 4 cups)
Pumpkin, cooked & mashed	300 g	0.66 lbs (approx. 1¼ cups)
Olive oil	60 ml	¼ cup
Bone broth	500 ml	2 cups
Crushed eggshell or calcium powder (optional)	As needed	As needed

Instructions:

Simmer chicken in broth until cooked. Stir in oats, carrots, and pumpkin. Add oil last. Cool, portion, and freeze.

Beef and Barley Energy Mix

Yields: ~5 kg / 11 lbs

Ingredient	Metric	Imperial
Lean beef mince	2 kg	4.4 lbs
Cooked pearl barley	1.5 kg	3.3 lbs (approx. 7 cups)
Zucchini, diced	500 g	1.1 lbs (approx. 4 cups)
Sweet potato, mashed	500 g	1.1 lbs (approx. 2 cups)
Flaxseed oil	60 ml	¼ cup
Parsley, chopped	1 tbsp	1 tbsp

Instructions: Brown beef lightly. Mix in cooked barley, vegetables, and sweet potato. Stir in flaxseed oil and parsley before cooling.

Sardines and Rice Digestive Mix

Yields: ~5 kg / 11 lbs

Ingredient	Metric	Imperial
Tinned sardines (in water)	1.5 kg (drained)	3.3 lbs (approx. 6 tins)
Cooked white rice	2 kg	4.4 lbs (approx. 9 cups)
Carrots, finely grated	500 g	1.1 lbs (approx. 4 cups)
Spinach, lightly steamed	250 g	½ lb (approx. 2 cups chopped)
Pumpkin purée	300 g	0.66 lbs (approx. 1¼ cups)
Coconut oil	60 ml	¼ cup

Instructions: Mash sardines and mix with all ingredients. Ideal for sensitive tummies or high-omega-3 support.

Chunky Lamb Stew

Ingredient	Metric	Imperial
Lamb chunks (neck, shoulder, offcuts)	2.5 kg	5.5 lbs
Carrots, chunky diced	500 g	1.1 lbs (approx. 4 cups)
Sweet potato, chopped	500 g	1.1 lbs (approx. 2½ cups)
Zucchini, thick-sliced	400 g	0.9 lbs (approx. 3 cups)
Cooked pearl barley	1 kg	2.2 lbs (approx. 5 cups)
Bone broth or water	1–1.2 litres	4–5 cups
Olive oil or flaxseed oil	60 ml	¼ cup
Parsley (optional)	1 tbsp	1 tbsp chopped

Instructions:

- Sear the lamb chunks in a large pot with a splash of water or oil until browned (optional but adds flavour).

- Add the vegetables and bone broth. Bring to a simmer.

- Cook on low for 1.5–2 hours, or until meat is tender and veggies are soft but chunky.

- Stir in the cooked barley and oil.

- Cool thoroughly. Portion and refrigerate or freeze.

Light meal mix

Yields: ~5 kg / 11 lbs

Ideal as a budget-friendly meat-light mix

Ingredient	Metric	Imperial
Eggs (boiled or scrambled)	2 dozen	24 eggs
Cooked lentils	1 kg	2.2 lbs (approx. 5 cups)
Rolled oats (cooked)	1.5 kg	3.3 lbs (approx. 6–7 cups)
Mixed veggies (carrot, zucchini, spinach)	1 kg	2.2 lbs (approx. 6 cups)
Flaxseed oil or coconut oil	60 ml	¼ cup
Calcium powder or crushed eggshell (optional)	–	–

Instructions: Chop or mash eggs and mix with lentils, oats, and veg. Stir in oil before cooling.

Weights Feeding Tip

Serve:

- Small dogs (under 10 kg): ½–¾ cup per meal

- Medium dogs (10–25 kg): 1–2 cups

- Large dogs (25–40 kg): 2–3 cups

- Giant dogs (40+ kg): 3–4 cups

Always adjust based on activity, age, and body condition.

Chapter 36

Kid-approved recipes

Safe, fun meals little hands can help make

Letting kids help prepare food for dogs builds empathy, responsibility, and joy, plus it's a whole lot of fun. These recipes are simple, safe, and involve minimal knives, ovens, or hot pans, but maximum excitement.

Doggy Shepherd's Pie (Kid spoon version)

- ½ cup cooked ground beef

- ½ cup mixed steamed veggies (peas, carrots, green beans)

- ½ cup mashed sweet potato

Instructions:

- Let kids layer beef on the bottom of a small dog-safe dish.

- Spoon veggies on top.

- Cover with a mashed sweet potato "crust" and a sprinkle of parsley.

- Serve slightly warm or cool.

Best for: special meals, reward days

Shephard's pie made by my grandson who loves to cook.

No-Bake Carrot Energy Balls

- ½ cup rolled oats (finely ground)

- ½ cup grated carrot

- 1 tablespoon peanut butter (xylitol-free)

- 1 tablespoon plain yoghurt

Instructions:

- Mix all ingredients in a bowl until sticky.

- Roll into tiny balls using clean hands.

- Chill in fridge for 30 minutes before serving.

Best for: Training treats, playdate snacks

Chicken and Rice Mini Muffins

- 1 cup cooked, shredded chicken
- ½ cup cooked rice
- 1 egg
- 2 tablespoons grated zucchini

Instructions:

- Mix all ingredients well.
- Spoon into silicone mini muffin trays.
- Bake at 180°C (350°F) for 15 minutes until firm.

Best for: Small reward bites, freezer stocking

Tuna and Spinach Dog Biscuits

- 1 tin tuna in spring water (drained)
- 1 cup oat flour (or blended rolled oats)
- ¼ cup steamed spinach (chopped)
- 1 egg

Instructions:

- Mash tuna with spinach.
- Stir in egg and oat flour.
- Roll into balls and flatten slightly.
- Bake at 160°C (320°F) for 20 minutes.

Best for: Omega boost snacks, dental crunch

Banana and Blueberry Quick Bites

- 1 ripe banana (mashed)
- ¼ cup blueberries (fresh or frozen)
- ½ cup oat flour

Instructions:

- Mix all ingredients gently.
- Form small blobs on a baking sheet.
- Bake at 160°C (320°F) for 15–20 minutes until firm.

Best for: Summer treats, puppy parties

Want a frozen treat idea?

Blend yoghurt + banana + blueberries. Pour into moulds, freeze, and you've got a summer snack.

Kid-friendly reminders:

- Always supervise young helpers with mixing and baking.
- Use plain, dog-safe ingredients (no chocolate chips, sugar, nuts, or artificial sweeteners).
- Let kids name their creations. It makes it extra special!

Chapter 37

Grandma's classics

Old-fashioned, hearty dog meals

B efore commercial kibble, dogs ate real food from the kitchen; scraps, broths, humble meals made with love. These classic recipes bring that wholesome tradition back in a safe, modern way. These meals store beautifully. Refrigerate up to 3 days or freeze in small batches.

Beef and Barley Stew

- 500g stewing beef, diced
- 1 cup pearl barley
- 1 cup diced carrots
- ½ cup chopped celery
- 2½ cups low-sodium bone broth or water

Instructions:

- Brown beef lightly (optional).
- Simmer beef, barley, and veggies together until soft (~2 hours).
- Cool before serving.

Best for: Strong muscles, cold weather comfort meals

Chicken Bone Broth Boost

- 2–3 chicken frames or necks (raw)
- 2 carrots (roughly chopped)
- 1 celery stick (roughly chopped)
- 2–3 litres water
- Splash of apple cider vinegar (helps pull minerals)

Instructions:

- Simmer all ingredients very gently for 8–12 hours.
- Strain carefully. Remove all bones before feeding broth!
- Cool and serve as a topper or drink.

Best for:

Joint support, hydration, post-surgery recovery

Scrambled Eggs and Spinach Mash

- 2 eggs
- 1 handful baby spinach (chopped)
- 1 teaspoon coconut oil

Instructions:

- Melt coconut oil in a pan.
- Scramble eggs lightly with spinach until just set.
- Cool slightly before serving.

Best for:

Sensitive tummies, fast energy meals

Liver and Veggie Bake

- 250g beef or lamb liver (finely chopped)
- 1 cup mashed sweet potato
- ½ cup peas
- 1 egg

Instructions:

- Mix all ingredients together.
- Spread into a shallow baking dish.
- Bake at 180°C (350°F) for 25–30 minutes until firm.
- Cut into squares once cooled.

Best for: Iron boost treats, anaemic or recovering dogs, adding variety.

Liver and veggie bake

Grandma's Chicken and Rice Casserole

- 1 cup cooked shredded chicken
- 1 cup cooked brown rice

- ½ cup mixed peas and carrots

- 1 teaspoon flaxseed oil

Instructions:

- Mix everything together while still slightly warm.

- Serve in small portions.

Best for: Everyday maintenance meals, mild appetite days

Ruby patiently waiting for dinner. Those eyes!

Chapter 38

Treats

Everyday biscuits and simple, crunchy treats

These are your dependable everyday rewards. Not too rich, not too messy, but loved by nearly every dog. Most recipes freeze beautifully and make wonderful gifts too. Cool treats completely before storing, refrigerate for 5 days, or freeze for longer freshness. Adjust size depending on your dog's jaw strength and chewing habits.

Peanut Butter and Oat Biscuits

- 1 cup oat flour (or finely blended rolled oats)

- ½ cup xylitol-free peanut butter

- 1 egg

- Splash of water (if needed)

Instructions:

- Mix peanut butter and egg first, then add oat flour.

- Form into small balls and flatten slightly.

- Bake at 160°C (320°F) for 12–15 minutes until firm.

Best for: Training rewards, light chewing snacks

Carrot and Apple Chews

- 1 small grated carrot
- ½ apple (grated, no seeds or core)
- 1 cup oat flour
- 1 egg

Instructions:

- Combine all ingredients gently.
- Spoon onto a lined tray.
- Bake at 160°C (320°F) for 20 minutes.

Best for:

Puppy snacks, dental-friendly chews

Sweet Potato Crisps

- 1 small sweet potato (cooked and mashed)
- 1 cup oat flour
- 1 tablespoon flaxseed meal
- 1 egg

Instructions:

- Blend all ingredients into a thick dough.
- Roll into logs or coin shapes.
- Bake at 160°C (320°F) for 25 minutes.

Best for:

Gut-soothing treats, older dogs

Sardine Crunch Bites

- 1 tin sardines in water (drained)
- 1 cup oat or chickpea flour
- 1 egg

Instructions:

1. Mash sardines first.

2. Mix in egg and flour until sticky.

3. Roll into tiny balls.

4. Bake at 160°C (320°F) for 15–18 minutes.

Best for:

Omega-3 snack, coat shine boosters

Cheesy Pumpkin Drops

- ½ cup pumpkin puree
- ½ cup grated low-fat cheese (like mozzarella)
- 1 cup oat flour

Instructions:

- Mix pumpkin and cheese first.
- Stir in flour to form dough.
- Drop spoonfuls onto tray.
- Bake at 160°C (320°F) for 15 minutes.

Best for: High-reward training treats

Using silicone trays for dog treats

Cheesy pumpkin treats

Chapter 39

Training treats

Little rewards for big learning moments

Training treats should be small, soft enough to eat quickly, and super appealing without being heavy. These are designed for fast delivery. No long chewing, no distractions!

Chicken and Cheese Quick Bites

- 1 cup cooked shredded chicken
- ½ cup grated mozzarella cheese
- 1 egg
- 1 tablespoon oat flour

Instructions:

- Mix chicken, cheese, and egg first.
- Stir in flour to bind slightly.
- Spoon tiny blobs onto tray.
- Bake at 160°C (320°F) for 10–12 minutes.

Best for:

Recall training, high-focus sessions

Tuna Training Nibbles

- 1 tin tuna in spring water (drained)
- 1 egg
- ½ cup oat or coconut flour

Instructions:

- Blend tuna and egg together.
- Mix in flour to form sticky dough.
- Shape into mini balls.
- Bake at 160°C (320°F) for 10 minutes.

Best for:

Scent work rewards, water-loving dogs

Sweet Potato Star Bits

- ½ cup cooked sweet potato (mashed)
- ½ cup oat flour
- 1 tablespoon flaxseed meal
- 1 egg

Instructions:

- Blend all ingredients together.
- Roll flat and cut with tiny cookie cutters (stars, bones, hearts!).
- Bake at 160°C (320°F) for 12–15 minutes.

Best for:

Young puppies, sensitive stomachs

Liver Boost Drops

- 100g beef or lamb liver (cooked and finely minced)

- 1 cup oat flour

- 1 egg

Instructions:

- Mash liver with egg.

- Stir in flour to bind.

- Drop tiny dots onto tray.

- Bake at 160°C (320°F) for 10 minutes.

Best for:

High-value training rewards, focus building

Training Treat Tips:

- Keep treats soft for easy, quick swallowing.

- Use pea-sized portions. Training is about repetition, not snacks!

- Store in fridge for 5–7 days or freeze for long-term freshness.

Sheltie Jasmin with her birthday cake, and yoghurt 'frosting.' (see p 205)

Chapter 40

Dental-friendly chews

Natural helpers for clean, strong teeth

C hewing isn't just fun for dogs. It's essential for oral health, jaw strength, and even mental relaxation. These recipes offer safe, digestible options that also scrub teeth while they chew.

Dehydrated Beef Strips

- 500g lean beef strips (thinly sliced)

Instructions:

- Lay beef slices on a lined baking tray.
- Bake at 80°C (175°F) for 6–8 hours until thoroughly dried.
- Cool and store in airtight jar.

Best for:

Medium to strong chewers

Chicken Jerky Strips

- 500g chicken breast (thinly sliced)

Instructions:

- Place chicken strips onto baking rack.
- Bake at 90°C (200°F) for 3–4 hours, flipping halfway.
- Cool completely before storing.

Best for:

Gentle chewing, skin and coat health

Parsley and Mint Dental Biscuits

- 1 cup oat flour
- ½ cup chopped fresh parsley
- ¼ cup chopped fresh mint
- 1 egg
- 1 tablespoon coconut oil

Instructions:

- Mix all ingredients into firm dough.
- Roll out and cut into small shapes.
- Bake at 160°C (320°F) for 20 minutes.

Best for:

Breath freshening, mild tartar control

Eggshell Crunch Bites

- 4-5 eggshells, cleaned and dried to a fine powder. (Bake 15 mins at 110°C (230°F)). Cool then grind finely with coffee grinder or blender.

- 1 cup plain yoghurt

Instructions:

- Mix into yoghurt

- Spoon into an icecube tray and freeze until solid.

- Offer frozen for crunch. Crush ice for small dogs or puppies

Best for: Calcium boost

Sweet Potato Chew Slices

- 1 large sweet potato

Instructions:

- Slice sweet potato lengthwise into 0.5cm (¼ inch) strips.

- Bake at 120°C (250°F) for 2–3 hours until dry but slightly flexible.

- Cool completely before offering.

Best for: Puppies teething, light chewers

Dental-friendly Chew Tips:

- Always supervise chewing to prevent gulping or choking.

- Introduce dehydrated treats slowly if your dog is new to tough textures.

- Offer fresh drinking water during and after chewing sessions.

Cold banana treat with yogurt, for summer.

Chapter 41

Gut-soothing snacks

Gentle treats for sensitive stomachs

T hese treats are designed with easy-to-digest ingredients, mild flavours, and a focus on gut balance. They're ideal after illness, antibiotics, or just for pups with more delicate digestion.

Start small. Sensitive tummies need to "trial" new treats. Use moist textures for easier digestion. Avoid raw bones, fatty cuts, and dairy (except plain probiotic yoghurt or kefir).

Rice and Chicken Squares

- ½ cup cooked white rice

- ½ cup cooked chicken (shredded)

- 1 egg

- 1 tablespoon parsley (finely chopped)

Instructions:

- Mix all ingredients together.

- Press into a lined baking tin and bake at 170°C (340°F) for 20 minutes.

- Cool and cut into squares.

Best for: Simple, bland, recovery-friendly treats

Pumpkin and Oat Biscuits

- ½ cup pumpkin puree (plain)
- 1 cup oat flour
- 1 tablespoon flaxseed meal
- 1 egg

Instructions:

- Combine ingredients into a dough.
- Roll into balls or flatten slightly.
- Bake at 160°C (320°F) for 20 minutes.

Best for: Soothing the gut lining, mild fibre boost

Frozen Yoghurt Drops

- ½ cup plain Greek yoghurt
- 1 teaspoon honey (optional)
- 1 tablespoon crushed blueberries or grated apple

Instructions:

- Stir all ingredients together.
- Spoon into silicone moulds or ice cube trays.
- Freeze for 2 hours. Pop out and serve chilled.

Best for: Hot weather, post-tummy bug recovery

Blueberry and Banana Bites

- 1 ripe banana (mashed)
- ¼ cup blueberries (fresh or frozen)
- ½ cup oat flour

Instructions:

- Mash banana and mix with berries and flour.
- Drop spoonfuls onto tray.
- Bake at 160°C (320°F) for 15 minutes.

Best for:

Antioxidant boost, sweet but mild treat

Ginger and Pumpkin Chews

- ½ cup pumpkin puree
- ½ teaspoon ground ginger
- 1 egg
- 1 cup oat flour

Instructions:

- Combine all ingredients until smooth.
- Roll into bite-sized shapes.
- Bake at 160°C (320°F) for 18–20 minutes.

Best for:

Dogs prone to nausea, mild bloating or car sickness

Action step:

Start with just one gut-soothing snack. Watch your dog's digestion over 24–48 hours, and if things improve, introduce no more than one at a time. Keep a note of what works best.

Gut healing takes time, particularly during post-antibiotic care, but even small adjustments can lead to more solid stools, less gas, and a calmer, happier dog.

Biscuits are best kept in an airtight glass container.

Chapter 42

Special occasion goodies

Celebration treats for your best friend

B irthdays, adoption days, first day of training, or just a "you're a good dog" moment, these treats are made for memory-making. They're a little more festive, a little more indulgent, but still gentle, safe, and made with love.

Doggy Birthday Cake

- 1 cup oat flour

- 1 egg

- ¼ cup peanut butter (xylitol-free)

- ¼ cup unsweetened applesauce

- ½ teaspoon baking powder

- Optional: 2 tablespoons grated carrot or apple

Instructions:

- Mix all ingredients into a batter.

- Pour into a small cake tin or ramekin.

- Bake at 170°C (340°F) for 20–25 minutes.

- Cool and top with yoghurt "frosting."

Yoghurt Frosting:

- Mix 2 tablespoons plain Greek yoghurt with a teaspoon of peanut butter or mashed banana.

Best for: Celebrations, photos, human-pup parties

Mini Pupcakes

- 1 ripe banana (mashed)

- 1 egg

- ¼ cup oat flour

- 1 tablespoon flaxseed

- Optional: pinch of cinnamon

Instructions:

- Mix all ingredients into a smooth batter.

- Spoon into silicone mini muffin trays.

- Bake at 160°C (320°F) for 12–15 minutes.

Best for: Dog party favours, freezer stash for birthdays

Celebration Doughnuts

- 1 cup oat flour

- 1 egg

- ½ cup unsweetened applesauce

- 1 tablespoon melted coconut oil

Instructions:

- Mix ingredients and spoon into doughnut moulds (or roll into rings).

- Bake at 170°C (340°F) for 15–18 minutes.

- Cool and decorate with dog-safe icing (see below).

Dog-Safe Icing Ideas:

- Plain yoghurt with beetroot powder

- Mashed banana + coconut cream

- Tinted kefir with blueberry juice

Best for: Sharing with furry friends, extra special days

Bone-Shaped Celebration Biscuits

- 1 cup wholemeal flour or oat flour

- ½ cup pumpkin puree

- 1 egg

- 1 tablespoon honey (optional for older dogs)

Instructions:

- Mix to form a dough.

- Roll and cut with bone-shaped cutters.

- Bake at 160°C (320°F) for 20 minutes.

Best for: Party bags, "treat table" showpieces

Frozen Birthday Cubes

- ½ cup kefir or Greek yoghurt

- ½ banana (mashed) or scoops of watermelon

- A few blueberries or strawberries

Instructions:

- Mix ingredients gently.

- Spoon into ice cube trays, mini muffin trays or bone moulds.

- Freeze and serve as frosty party snacks.

Best for: Hot weather birthdays, senior dogs who love cool treats

---

Birthday treat notes:

- All recipes are share-safe for multiple dogs.

- Store cakes and pup-cakes in the fridge for 3–4 days, or freeze left-overs.

- Always supervise new textures and toppings. Excitement can equal fast gobbling!

Chapter 43

Final thoughts

A nourishing life together

As you turn these final pages, take a moment to recognise the journey you've walked, not just through the chapters of this book, but into a more conscious, connected way of caring for your dog.

Whether you arrived here as a cautious beginner, a frustrated label-reader, or just curious about wanting something more wholesome than another bag of biscuits, you've made it to a place of deeper understanding.

You now know how to:

- Prepare balanced, nourishing meals from your own kitchen

- Adjust for life stages and sensitivities

- Choose ingredients and feeding styles that suit your dog, and your lifestyle

- Read your dog's body language, appetite, energy, and behaviour as feedback

- And maybe most importantly... trust your instincts, even while learning

Fat doesn't mean healthy

It's not always easy to say, and it's certainly not easy to hear, but many beloved dogs are overweight. Not just a little soft around the edges, but carrying serious, chronic extra weight that will shorten their lives, compromise their joints, and leave them slower, stiffer, and more uncomfortable than they ever need to be.

We love our dogs. But too often, that love gets expressed through food. A little something from the dinner plate. A spoonful of yoghurt. A bedtime biscuit. A handful of dry food that's just a bit over the serving size. A few dropped scraps here and there. It all adds up. And unfortunately, your dog's body doesn't forget.

Most people don't know what a healthy dog body looks like. But it's not barrel-shaped. You should be able to feel your dog's ribs easily, without pressing or digging. In short-haired breeds, you should even see two or three ribs when they breathe out after exercise. If you can't, your dog is likely carrying too much weight.

And no, "fat but happy" is not a valid argument. A dog that's heavier than it should be is at risk of joint pain, arthritis, diabetes, heart strain, breathing issues, fatty liver disease, and more. Extra fat doesn't mean extra love. It means stress. On their skeleton, their organs, and their quality of life.

Where the weight comes from

Most of the time, overweight dogs are not the result of a health condition. They are the result of overfeeding and under-exercising. That's it. No magic. No mystery.

Even well-meaning owners can overfeed by:

- Giving table scraps "just this once"

- Letting the dog lick dishes or clean up dropped food

- Adding toppers or extras to meals without adjusting quantities

- Allowing others in the house to feed the dog without asking

- Allowing the dog to scavenge outside

If you're not the one controlling every single bite that goes into your dog's mouth, it's almost impossible to keep them at a healthy weight. It's not harsh. It's necessary.

What to do about it

If your dog is overweight, the solution is simple. Feed less and move more. Reduce portions. Skip the extras. Cut out treats unless they're counted into the daily total. Try to increase movement. Even a little helps. A short daily walk is better than nothing. A few ball tosses in the yard make a difference.

Feed your dog based on the weight they should be, not the weight they are now. Most feeding guides print maximum portions, not tailored recommendations. And don't rely on those wide-eyed stares at dinnertime. Dogs are wired to accept food. That doesn't mean they need it.

Your dog is counting on you

Your dog can't measure their own food. They can't open the fridge. They can't check the scale or ask for a smaller portion. They rely on you to be the one who sets the standard, with calm consistency and care.

That doesn't mean punishment or guilt. It means informed decisions made with love.

If you've slipped into habits that are adding extra weight to your dog, you're not alone. But you can change course. And you can do it gently. No dog needs to go hungry or feel deprived. They need balance, predictability, and food that suits their body and lifestyle. Not yours.

Feeding well means feeding wisely. And feeding wisely means keeping them lean, mobile, and feeling their best.

Because love isn't measured in scoops. It's measured in years.

This book wasn't just about food. It was about relationship. About choosing, every day, to do right by your dog in ways big and small, and understanding that "right" doesn't mean perfect. It means: *I see you. I love you.*

As we wrap up this journey, remember that you are not alone. You have the tools, knowledge, and support to succeed. The path to homemade dog meals is rewarding and ongoing. Embrace it with enthusiasm and curiosity.

Wherever you go from here, keep going. Keep learning, trying, adapting. Your confidence will grow. Let mistakes be small, laughter be loud, and recipes be forgiving.

And remember: your dog doesn't need a professional chef. They need *you*. Present. Willing. Learning as you go.

Thank you for allowing me to be part of your journey. Together, we've explored a world of homemade dog food that promises health and happiness for your beloved pet.

Here's to many more meals shared with love and care. Keep cooking, keep learning, and most importantly, keep enjoying the special bond you share with your dog.

Warmly ~ Jeanette

We hope you have enjoyed this journey together

APPENDICES

Troubleshooting

Recommended Reading:
Raw fed and nerdy. Website: https://rawfedandnerdy.com/

Homemade dog food recipes
Facebook: https://www.facebook.com/groups/3811403639186117

Dogs First is the home of Dr Conor Brady, author of the top-rated canine nutrition book *Feeding Dogs*:
Facebook: https://www.facebook.com/DogsFirstIreland

Appendix A: Conversion charts (grams/ounces, cups, portions)

Dog Type	Daily Feed Amount	Daily Feed Amount (Imperial)
Puppies	5–8% of body weight/day	2–3.5 oz per 5 lb/day
Adults	2–3% of body weight/day	1–1.5 oz per 5 lb/day
Seniors	1.5–2.5% of body weight/day	0.75–1.25 oz per 5 lb/day
Working Dogs	3–5% of body weight/day	1.5–2.5 oz per 5 lb/day
Weight Loss Plan	1.5–2% of body weight/day	0.75–1 oz per 5 lb/day

Quick serving examples:

- A 10kg (22 lb) adult dog would eat roughly 200–300g (7–10 oz) of food per day.

- A 25kg (55 lb) active dog might need 750g–1.25kg (1.7–2.7 lb) daily.

Weight Conversions

Metric (g/kg)	Imperial (oz/lb)
5g	0.18 oz
10g	0.35 oz
50g	1.76 oz
100g	3.5 oz
250g	8.8 oz
500g	17.6 oz / 1.1 lb
1kg	2.2 lb

Volume Conversions

Volume (Metric)	Approx. Imperial Equivalent
1 teaspoon (tsp)	5 ml
1 tablespoon (tbsp)	15 ml
¼ cup	60 ml
½ cup	120 ml
1 cup	240 ml (8 fl oz)
1 litre	4.2 cups / 34 fl oz

Measurements Quick Reference

Ingredient	1 Cup = Approx. Grams	Notes
Cooked rice	200g	Firmly packed
Pumpkin purée	225g	No sugar/spice added
Oat flour	90g	Lightly spooned, not packed
Shredded chicken	140g	Cooked, finely chopped
Minced meat	250g	Raw
Bone broth	240ml	1 cup
Yoghurt (plain)	240g	1 cup

Appendix B: Conversion measures

This reference helps convert measurements between cups, grams, ounces, and cooked vs. raw volumes. All values are approximate and intended for everyday use.

Dry to cooked yields (grains and legumes)

- White rice: ½ cup dry = approx.1½ cups cooked

- Brown rice: ½ cup dry = approx.1½ to 1¾ cups cooked

- Pearl barley: ½ cup dry =approx. 1½ cups cooked

- Quinoa: ¼ cup dry = approx. ¾cup cooked

- Rolled oats: ½ cup dry =approx. 1 to 1¼ cups cooked

- Lentils (brown or green): ½ cup dry = approx. 1 to 1¼ cups cooked

Common ingredient weight equivalents

- 1 cup cooked white rice: 200 g/ 7 oz

- 1 cup mashed sweet potato: 200 g / 7 oz

- 1 cup cooked rolled oats: 230 g/ 8 oz

- 1 cup cooked quinoa: 185 g /6.5 oz

- 1 cup cooked lentils: 198 g / 7oz

- 1 cup chopped chicken (cooked):140 g / 5 oz

- 1 medium sweet potato: 180–200 g / 6.5–7 oz

Liquid conversions

- 1 cup: 240 ml / 8 fl oz

- ½ cup: 120 ml / 4 fl oz

- ¼ cup: 60 ml / 2 fl oz

- 1 tbsp: 15 ml / 0.5 fl oz

- 1 tsp: 5 ml / 0.17 fl oz

Daily food portions by dog weight

These are general daily food amounts. Adjust for age, energy, and health.

- 2–5 kg: 50–150 g (2–5 oz) - toy breeds like Chihuahua, Maltese, mini Dachshund

- 6–10 kg: 150–300 g (5–10 oz) – mini Schnauzer, Cavalier, Fox Terrier, Dachshund

- 11–20 kg: 300–600 g (10–21 oz) - Cocker Spaniel, Kelpie, Border Collie

- 21–30 kg: 600–850 g (21–30 oz) - Staffy, Labrador, Bulldog

- 31–40 kg: 850 g–1.2 kg (30–42oz) - Golden Retriever, Husky, German Shepherd

- 41–50 kg: 1.2–1.5 kg (42–53 oz) - Doberman, Ridgeback, Rottweiler

- 51 kg+: 1.5–2 kg+ (53–70 oz+) – Great Dane, Mastiff, Wolfhound

Appendix C: Substitution guide:

Handy swaps when you're short

Use this quick guide when you're missing an ingredient in a recipe. These substitutions are safe for dogs and keep your meal balanced and digestible. Always ensure substitutions are plain, unsalted and cooked where needed.

- Chicken mince: Turkey mince (same amount)

- Pumpkin (cooked or purée): Mashed sweet potato (1:1 ratio)

- Sweet potato: Cooked butternut squash or pumpkin (1:1 ratio)

- Rolled oats (cooked): Cooked brown rice or quinoa (same amount, cooked)

- Beef mince: Lamb mince or turkey mince (same amount)

- Tinned sardines: Tinned mackerel or salmon in water (same amount)

- Bone broth: Plain water with a splash of apple cider vinegar (2 tbsp per litre)

- Coconut oil: Olive oil or flaxseed oil (same amount)

- Zucchini: Green beans or finely cut parsnip (1:1 ratio)

- Eggs: ¼ cup cottage cheese or plain yoghurt per egg (approximate volume)

- Broccoli: Chopped spinach or steamed cauliflower (1:1 ratio)

- Cauliflower: Mashed potato (plain) or pumpkin (less gas-forming; use ¾ amount)

- Meat: Lentils can be used in place of part of the meat in a meal (for variety or lower cost), or grains like rice or oats, especially in sensitive dogs who tolerate legumes better

Appendix D: Ingredient glossary

Animal Proteins

Beef
A classic red meat, rich in iron, zinc, and B12. Use lean cuts or mince (ground) for best digestion. Too much fat can cause tummy upsets.

Chicken
A mild, digestible protein for most dogs. Use boneless, skinless cuts. Chicken thighs and breasts are ideal for everyday meals.

Duck
Higher in fat than chicken, but rich in flavour and iron. Best used in moderation or for dogs needing extra calories.

Eggs
High in protein and biotin. Can be served cooked or raw (use yolk only if raw). Great for coat health and energy.

Fish (e.g., sardines, white fish)
Excellent source of omega-3s and lean protein. Use boneless, cooked fish or raw sardines/tinned in water. Frames only for larger dogs.

Goat
A lean, hypoallergenic meat often tolerated by dogs with sensitivities. Rich in iron and amino acids.

Kangaroo
Exceptionally lean, wild game meat. High in iron and zinc. Ideal for allergy-friendly diets.

Lamb
A rich red meat with healthy fats. Cook well and trim excess fat. Great in rotation with other proteins.

Pork
Flavourful but fatty. Use lean pork cuts and cook thoroughly. No processed ham or bacon.

Rabbit
Lean, low-fat, and ideal for dogs with allergies. Best served cooked and boneless.

Turkey
Mild and lower-fat than chicken. Turkey mince or thigh meat is ideal. Can have a calming effect in some dogs.

Venison
Nutrient-dense meat, high in iron, low in fat. Ideal for allergy-prone dogs.

Grains and Seeds

Barley
Slow-digesting carbohydrate with fibre and minerals. Cook well. Great for sustained energy.

Brown Rice
Whole grain with fibre and minerals. Needs thorough cooking. May be harder to digest for some dogs than white rice.

Hemp Seeds
Omega-3 and protein boost. Feed ground or soaked. Best used sparingly.

Oats (Rolled)
Mild, soluble fibre source. Cook before feeding. Helps regulate digestion.

Pearl Barley
Easier to cook and digest than hulled barley. Ideal in stews and slow-cooked meals.

Pumpkin Seeds (Pepitas)
Rich in zinc and healthy fats. Feed ground or soaked. Use in moderation. Too many = excess fat.

Oils, Liquids, and Additions

Bone Broth
Collagen-rich liquid made from simmered bones. Supports joints, digestion, and hydration. No onion or salt!

Coconut Oil
Antimicrobial and energy-boosting fat. Use in small amounts to avoid loose stools.

Flaxseed / Flaxseed Oil (Linseed)
Good source of plant-based omega-3s. Use ground seeds or cold-pressed oil. Helpful for skin, coat, and digestion.

Kefir
Fermented milk with live probiotics. Supports gut health. Use plain, unsweetened only.

Olive Oil
Safe in small amounts. Rich in monounsaturated fats. Adds shine to coat.

Plain Yoghurt
Natural probiotic. Use plain, unsweetened varieties only. Avoid if lactose-intolerant.

Salmon / Fish Oil
High in EPA and DHA (omega-3s). Great for joints, brain, and skin health. Dose conservatively.

Vegetables

Asian greens (like bok choy, choy sum, wombok/napa cabbage)
Safe in small amounts, especially steamed or lightly cooked. These are low-oxalate, non-gassy alternatives to kale or spinach, and often more affordable. Chop finely and avoid seasoning.

Beetroot
Rich in folate and fibre. Steam or roast before feeding. Serve in moderation due to natural sugars.

Bell Peppers / Capsicum
Safe in small amounts. Best cooked (steamed or roasted). Remove seeds and white membrane.

Broccoli
Contains antioxidants and fibre. Steam lightly. Serve in moderation to avoid gas.

Carrot
Great raw (for chewing) or cooked. High in beta carotene and fibre. Watch for choking hazard in raw chunks. Parsnip can be a substitute.

Cauliflower
Safe, but use in moderation. It should be fed steamed or lightly cooked to make it easier to digest. Cauliflower is high in fibre and antioxidants but can cause gas in some dogs if overused.

Cucumber
Safe and hydrating. Serve raw without skins and chopped. Contains vitamins B and C and is very low calorie, making it a good summer snack or treat for overweight dogs.

Green Beans
Low-calorie, high-fibre veg. Best steamed or lightly cooked. Good filler for weight control meals.

Pumpkin
Excellent for digestion. Use plain cooked or canned purée (100% pumpkin). Not pumpkin pie filling!

Spinach
Rich in iron and magnesium. Lightly steam to remove oxalates before feeding.

Sweet Potato
Nutrient-rich, easily digestible carb. Cook and mash for gut-soothing meals.

Zucchini
Hydrating and mild. Lightly steamed or grated raw. A good low-calorie veg.

These are the most common and nutritious vegetables that work beautifully in homemade dog meals. Always serve steamed, blended, or finely chopped for better digestion.

Store-bought mushrooms: like button, cremini, and portobello are technically safe when cooked and fed in small amounts. Do not feed wild or foraged mushrooms.

Vegetable cooking guide

Vegetable	Safe Prep	Notes
Carrot	Raw or cooked, grated/sliced	Great for teeth and beta carotene
Sweet Potato	Cooked only (no skin)	Gut-soothing, rich in vitamin A
Pumpkin	Cooked or pureed (no spice)	Excellent for digestion
Zucchini	Raw or steamed	Low-calorie, hydrating
Broccoli	Lightly steamed only	Good in small amounts; can cause gas
Green Beans	Steamed or raw, chopped	Great filler, low-calorie
Spinach	Lightly steamed	High in iron; avoid excess due to oxalates
Beetroot	Boiled or roasted, no skin	High in fibre and folate; stain warning!
Celery	Finely chopped or steamed	Crunchy, good for breath, low-calorie
Cauliflower	Lightly steamed only	Use in moderation — can cause gas
Parsley	Finely chopped (curly only)	Freshens breath and supports kidneys

Fruits:

Banana
A soft, easy treat. High in potassium and fibre. Serve in small chunks. Can be mashed into biscuits or frozen with yoghurt.

Apple
Crunchy and refreshing. High in fibre and vitamin C. Remove the core and all seeds (which contain trace cyanide). Peel for sensitive tummies.

Pear
Mild and sweet. Peel and remove seeds and core. Rich in vitamin K and fibre. Serve chopped, not whole.

Peach and Nectarine
Juicy and full of antioxidants. Must remove pit (choking + cyanide risk). Chop into soft bites. Avoid canned fruit in syrup.

Cherries (Flesh only)
Cherry flesh is safe, but avoid pits, stems, and leaves. They contain cyanogenic compounds. Not ideal as a frequent snack.

Strawberries
Full of antioxidants and vitamin C. Slice or mash before serving. Limit if your dog is sensitive to sugars.

Blueberries
A true superfood for dogs. Rich in antioxidants, fibre, and gentle on digestion. Great frozen for warm days.

Melon (Rockmelon/Cantaloupe)
Hydrating and sweet. Remove rind and seeds. Serve chilled in chunks. Avoid if overly ripe or fermenting.

Watermelon
Very hydrating. Remove seeds and rind. Only offer flesh in small cubes. Excellent in ice treats.

Mango (Ripe only)
Peel and remove pit. Soft, fibrous fruit that's rich in vitamins. Some dogs find it too sweet. Feed sparingly.

Kiwi Fruit
Tart and fibrous. Skin can be irritating. Peel first. Offer only in small amounts to avoid mouth irritation.

Pineapple (Fresh only)
Contains bromelain (aids digestion). Remove tough core and prickly skin. High in sugar, small servings only.

Fruit Feeding Tips:

- Keep portions small (1–2 slices or cubes).

- Use fruits as treats, not meal replacements.

- Always remove seeds, pits, tough skin, and fermenting bits.

- Watch for loose stools with too much fruit.

Appendix E: Grain and starch cooking guide

Use this guide to safely prepare the most common grains and starches used in home-cooked dog meals. Always cook plain, without salt, oil, seasoning or stock. Let grains cool completely before serving. All can be cooked in advance and frozen for later to add to dishes.

Brown rice

- Rinse well.

- Use 1 part rice to 2½ parts water.

- Simmer covered for 35 to 40 minutes.

- Fluff and cool before feeding.

- Yield: ½ cup dry = approx. 1½ to 1¾ cups cooked.

Lentils (green or red) – pulses, chick peas

- Rinse thoroughly.

- Use 1 part lentils to 3 parts water.

- Simmer uncovered for 20 to 25 minutes until soft.

- Yield: ½ cup dry = approx. 1 to 1¼ cups cooked.

Pearl barley

- Use 1 part barley to 3 parts water.

- Simmer uncovered for 25 to 35 minutes until tender.

- Drain excess water and cool.

- Yield: ½ cup dry = approx. 1½ cups cooked.

Pepitas (pumpkin seeds)

Use raw, unsalted pepitas. Do not use seasoned, salty, or roasted snack versions made for humans.

- Lightly toast in a dry pan over low heat for 2 to 3 minutes, just until they start to pop.

- Cool completely

- Grind or chop before adding to meals.

Quinoa

Place quinoa in a fine strainer and rinse under running water for at least 30 seconds. This removes saponins, which can be bitter and cause stomach upset.

- Use 1 part quinoa to 2 parts water.

- Bring to a boil, then simmer for 15 to 20minutes until fluffy.

- Let cool before use.

- Yield: ¼ cup dry = approx. ¾ cup cooked.

Rolled oats

- Use 1 part oats to 2 parts water.

- Simmer gently for 5 to 10 minutes until soft.

- Cool completely before mixing.

- Yield: ½ cup dry = approx. 1 to 1¼ cups cooked.

Sweet potato

- Peel and cube.

- Steam or boil for 10 to 15 minutes until fork-tender.

- Mash or leave chunky. Cool before adding.

- Yield: 1 medium sweet potato = approx. 1 to 1½ cups cooked.

White rice

- Rinse briefly to remove excess starch.

- Use 1 part rice to 2 parts water.

- Simmer covered for 15 to 18 minutes.

- Cool before serving.

- Yield: ½ cup dry = approx. 1½ cups cooked.

Appendix F: Frequently asked questions

Q: Can I switch proteins every day?
A: Yes, if your dog has a stable gut. Otherwise, introduce new proteins every 3–5 days to monitor reactions.

Q: What if my dog skips a meal?
A: If they're healthy, it's okay! But repeated skipping could signal too much food, boredom, or an upset gut.

Q: Are raw eggs safe?
A: Yes, in moderation. One raw egg 2–3 times a week is fine for most dogs. Don't overdo it with dogs prone to biotin deficiency.

Q: My dog won't eat veggies. Now what?
A: Steam and blend them into meals, mix with broth or meat. Most dogs won't notice once it's part of the "gravy." Feed small amounts at first.

Q: Can I feed leftovers?
A: Only if unseasoned, low-fat, and dog-safe (no onion, garlic, sauces, or bones). Best to cook separately when in doubt.

Q: Can I feed my cat the same food as my dog?
A: No, not long term. Cats and dogs have very different nutritional needs. Cats are obligate carnivores, which means:

- They require much higher levels of taurine, an amino acid dogs can make on their own

- They need more protein and fat, and fewer carbohydrates

- They rely on animal-based vitamin A and arachidonic acid, both of which are often lacking in dog food

Feeding your cat dog meals occasionally *won't hurt them* in a pinch, but over time, it can lead to nutritional deficiencies, especially affecting the eyes, heart, and immune system. If you're feeding both **a** homemade diet, they'll need different recipes, even if the base ingredients look similar.

Q: Why do dogs eat grass?
A: It's often normal. They may enjoy the texture or use it to ease minor nausea. It's possibly linked to enzymes/chlorophyll in the grass which they like, but not necessarily a deficiency. Unless it's excessive, obsessive, or causing vomiting, it's not a concern. Make sure your grass isn't chemically treated.

Q: How long does cooked food last in the fridge?
A: Three days is a safe rule. If you're not going to use it all within that time, freeze in portion sizes as soon as it's cooled.

Q: Can I mix recipes together or rotate them during the week?
A: Yes. Dogs benefit from variety, especially when changes are made gradually.

Q: Do I need to add supplements to slow-cooked food?
A: That depends on the recipe. Most are balanced as a base, but you can add fish oil or calcium at serving.

Q: Can I feed slow-cooked food to puppies?
A: Yes, but use smaller portions more often. Put it through a blender for smaller pieces for little teeth. Choose higher-protein recipes and monitor growth.

Q: What's the best way to portion and store large batches?
A: Use large freezer safe bags or storage containers. Label with date and contents. Store in a chest freezer.

Q: What if my dog won't eat a new recipe?
A: Warm it slightly. Add broth or crumble a favourite treat on top. I have found sometimes that not giving them their next meal until they have cleaned it up is helpful. Just don't give into those pleading eyes for something different. If they only eat half of it, mix it with something they do like. Don't leave the food out *hoping* they will eat it. Put it out again at next mealtime. If still no, bin it.

Q: Can I reheat meals from the fridge or freezer?
A: Yes. Warm slightly and stir. Never serve hot.

Q: Are bones safe in these recipes?
A: Yes, but always remove them. Never serve cooked bones.

Q: What about brown rice or heritage varieties?
A: Brown rice is not unsafe for dogs. In fact, it's higher in fibre and nutrients like B vitamins and magnesium. But that fibre comes from the bran layer, which:

- Can be harder to digest, especially for dogs with gut sensitivities

- May interfere with nutrient absorption in some dogs if overfed

- Takes longer to cook, which can affect texture and how well dogs tolerate it

Some heritage or "ancient" grains like red rice, black rice, and wild rice are fine too, as long as they are cooked thoroughly, used in moderation, and introduced **slowly** if your dog hasn't had them before.

Q: Why white rice?
A: Although white rice has no nutritional value, it is often recommended because it is:

- More easily digested, especially for dogs with sensitive stomachs or recovering from illness

- A useful filler for overweight dogs

- Lower in fibre, which makes it gentler on the gut

- Less likely to trigger digestive upset, especially during food transitions or bland diet phases

- Faster to cook, softer in texture, suits older or dogs with dental issues

Q: Can corn be used?
A: Yes, in moderation. While corn isn't harmful to most dogs, it's often used as a bulk filler in commercial kibble, which gives it a bad name. Fresh or lightly cooked corn off the cob, can provide fibre, energy, and some antioxidants. Avoid processed or salty versions like canned corn with additives.

Q: Should I feed for variety and provide an egg and sardines 2x per week?
A: Basically you can, but always do what works for you and your dog.

Appendix G: Bonus – Checklist of gear to have on hand at whelping

Feeding Supplies

- Puppy feeding bottles (with tiny nipples) or 1 ml, 5 ml syringes
- Spare teats/nipples (very small size, slow flow)
- Tiny measuring cups/spoons (for accurate milk prep)
- Warm water bottle or electric bottle warmed

Temperature Control

- Safe, low-voltage heating pad (under bedding, not direct skin contact)
- Thermometer (to monitor the whelping area, aim for 29–32°C / 85–90°F in the first week)
- Room heater or heat lamp (safe distance to prevent burns)

Hygiene Essentials

- Puppy-safe sanitiser for hands
- Soft cloths or cotton pads (for cleaning mouths and stimulating toileting)
- Gentle puppy wipes (unscented)

Monitoring Tools

- Kitchen scale (digital, grams and ounces) to weigh pups daily
- Feeding log or notebook (record times, amounts, poops, weights)
- Clock or alarm for overnight feeding

Bedding & Nest

- Soft, washable bedding (fleece is best)
- Shallow box, basket, or whelping pen (draft-free, easy to access)

Index to Recipes

Help other dog owners like you. Leave a quick review!

Dear Reader,

A huge THANK YOU for picking up "Healthy Dog Food Recipes" I hope it's helping you gain clarity, confidence, and a game plan for your future!

Now, I'd love to ask a small (but meaningful) favour:

Could you take 2 minutes to leave an honest review?
Your feedback does 3 powerful things:

- Helps other enthusiastic dog lovers discover if this book is right for them.

- Supports me in creating more resources to help people like you succeed.

- Gives you a chance to reflect. What part of the book inspired or helped you most?

Please could you click the universal link below to leave your review on Amazon now:
https://mybook.to/homemade-dog-food

Every single review makes a difference, even just a sentence or two!
I am grateful for your support ~ Jeanette

P.S. Already left a review? You're amazing! Consider sharing the book with a friend who'd benefit from it or posting on your Facebook page.

INDEX TO RECIPES

If your dog could read this book, what recipe would he choose?

Also by Jeanette Gower

Jeanette is well known in equine circles as a breeder, educator, and published author. Her equine titles have helped thousands of horse owners and enthusiasts better understand horse behaviour, training, bloodlines, and responsible breeding. Her books reflect a clear, calm voice and the ability to make complex topics practical and accessible, qualities that carry effortlessly into her writing on dog nutrition.

If you've enjoyed this book, you may also enjoy Jeanette's equine writing. Follow her journey, explore her other titles (including TTHB audiobook), and stay updated by visiting Amazon OR you can support her by buying direct:

http://books.by/Jeanette-Gower

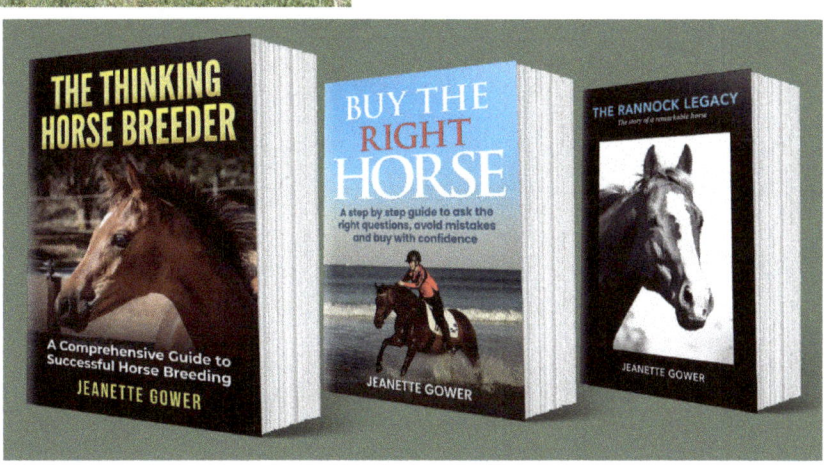

AUST. CH. CHALANI ERIN

Sable & White Bitch   **Born:** 29-9-80   **Title granted** 6-11-1981
Breeder: Mrs. J. T. Gower
Owner: Mrs. J. T. Gower, "Chalani", Box 73, Echunga, S.A. 5153.
Phone: (08) 388 8372

Aust. Ch. Kerondi Roving Love	Stormane Summer Rover (Imp. U.K.)	Stormane Shepherd
		Stormane Secret Pleasure
	Aust. Ch. Kerondi First Love	Aust. Ch. Rodanieh Rock Mundi (Imp. U.K.)
		Kerondi Latest Love
Ceston Jasmin	Aust. Ch. Kerondi Man About Town	Almaroy Adjudicate
		Aust. Ch. Hortonpark Pollyanna
	Kerondi Latest Love	Aust. Ch. Lisronagh Samba
		Aust. Ch. Kerondi Maid Marion

About the Author

Jeanette Gower is a long-time dog lover from South Australia and a strong believer in feeding dogs real food, without fuss, fear, or fads.

With decades of hands-on experience raising animals and working closely with dogs of all breeds, Jeanette has developed a practical, balanced approach to canine nutrition that blends common sense, nutritional grounding, and a dash of what you already have in your fridge.

Her experience with dogs began early. At just eight years old, she was already attending obedience classes with her first Shetland Sheepdog. That early love for training and connection continued through life. She has bred an Australian Champion Shetland Sheepdog and raised a joyful variety of dogs over the years, including Italian Greyhounds, Cattle Dogs, retired Greyhounds, and a lively Dachshund or two.

Her background spans a lifetime of animal husbandry, not only with dogs, but also as a respected breeder of horses and published author in the equine world. Jeanette's insights come from the paddock, the kitchen, *and* the show world.

As a writer, she's known for her clear, calm voice and her ability to make complex topics practical and readable. This background brings a grounded credibility to her work with dogs, and a steady hand to everything she writes.

Jeanette set out to create a resource that would make healthy, home-prepared dog meals achievable for everyone. She knew it had to be affordable, flexible, and grounded in trust. She doesn't push one strict diet model, and she's not here to scare you into throwing out your kibble.

Instead, she offers a guidebook for gradual change, gentle improvement, and choosing what works best for your dog and your household.

She believes feeding well is an act of care, one that should feel empowering, not intimidating. With calm guidance and real food, this book is her way of helping you do just that.

www.ingramcontent.com/pod-product-compliance
Lightning Source LLC
Chambersburg PA
CBHW051141120626
46547CB00012B/905